Shaping the Entrepreneurial Company

David McKeran
and Eric Flannigan

2000

First published in 1996 by Management Books 2000 Ltd
Cowcombe House,
Cowcombe Hill,
Chalford,
Gloucestershire GL6 8HP
(Tel: 01285-760722 Fax: 01285-760708)

Printed and bound in Great Britain by The Orbital Press, Letchworth

British Library Cataloguing in Publication Data is available

ISBN 1-85252-241-0 (paperback)

Foreword

For too long, the role of the entrepreneur and the entrepreneurial company in creating a country's prosperity in terms of jobs and wealth has been under-appreciated. The ability to spot and develop opportunities to create products and services of value and deliver them to customers has been taken for granted or, worse yet, totally disregarded.

Yet entrepreneurial activity is the prime mover of any economy and there are strong indications that a great wave of entrepreneurial behaviour is about to sweep through the world. Since taking up the post of Chief Executive at Scottish Enterprise, I have been determined that we create in Scotland a culture that is encouraging and supportive of entrepreneurialism.

I admit a certain pride in the way that individuals and companies have come forward to support the strategy we launched three years ago for *Improving the Business Birth Rate: A Strategy for Scotland*. I can only commend Eric Flannigan and David McKeran of Matrix for making an important contribution to increasing the understanding of the entrepreneurial company with this book. Eric and David have also relied heavily on examples drawn from Scottish companies – illustrating and confirming that the spirit of entrepreneurialism is alive and well in Scotland.

As I have said, there are many myths surrounding entrepreneurial companies. This book seeks to explode them. It tackles the mistaken belief that entrepreneurs are born, not made, by showing that much can be done to develop and hone entrepreneurial skill.

If you have ever equated smallness with entrepreneurialism, this book will also challenge your assumptions. David and Eric make a strong case that not all small companies, even those led by entrepreneurs, are necessarily entrepreneurial. They also show that growing a business does not mean that the company must eventually lose its entrepreneurial ethos and approach.

In doing so, David and Eric provide useful pointers to leaders of companies that are currently small and medium-sized on how to improve ability to think and act strategically and develop their leadership role by creating vision, purpose and goals for the growing organisation.

I applaud this book's contribution to the understanding of what it takes to create and foster the entrepreneurial company. The insights drawn from Scottish companies are clearly leading edge and stand up to challenge from anywhere else in the world. Matrix is part of a vanguard which places Scotland at the heart of entrepreneurial activity worldwide.

Crawford Beveridge
Chief Executive
Scottish Enterprise

Acknowledgements

This book is based on our work in Matrix Management Consultancy on the development of entrepreneurs and growing companies. We are fortunate in Matrix to have a team who are continually developing their experience and expertise in the growing company and have shared this with us. Special thanks are due to our partner Allan McLaughlin, who has worked with us to develop and shape many of the ideas contained in the book.

Many articles, reports and books have inspired our thinking and as these are too numerous to list, apart from those directly mentioned, we would like to thank all the authors concerned.

We would also like to thank the entrepreneurs who have contributed to this book; the clients who we have worked with; and those who agreed to be interviewed by us.

Contents

Part 1

Introduction to the Entrepreneurial Company

Chapter 1

Towards Enterprise – The Entrepreneurial Company

One venture capitalist described entrepreneurs as "arrogant, self-centred, self-opinionated egoists....who tend to take shortcuts, flaunt procedures and rarely work to the book". This description was not meant to be complimentary, concentrating on the more negative aspects of some entrepreneurial personalities. A more balanced view could well describe entrepreneurs as "innovative, focused, high achieving individuals....who tend to take shortcuts, flaunt procedures, rarely work to the book and accordingly develop some of the most innovative, profitable, fastest growing companies in our economy". The importance of the entrepreneur and the vibrant companies they create cannot be underestimated in any dynamic economy.

It is not surprising that in many countries, most obviously the USA, the entrepreneur is given hero status and successful entrepreneurs are paraded as role models to be emulated. Over the past decade in the UK there has been an increasing fascination with entrepreneurs and entrepreneurial behaviour. Government Agencies have started to become aware of the importance of this area, the media has publicised and popularised such high-profile entrepreneurs as Richard Branson and Anita Roddick, and large companies have tried to encourage entrepreneurial behaviour as a way of improving decreasing competitiveness. There is a general agreement that the entrepreneurial characteristics of flexibility, innovation and risk-taking are positive values which should be encouraged in all organisations.

In a wide-ranging report into the future of work, the Henley Centre for Forecasting examined the views of UK managers about the attributes of the ideal company of the future. A key attribute identified was in-built in mechanisms which allow rapid responses to changing customer needs. The report went on to state that "The responsive and flexible organisations of the future will have decentralised decision-making, devolved autonomy and independent work groups exchanging ideas and information in a loose informal structure". These characteristics suggest a need for a fundamental reappraisal of the attitudes of management and the structure of companies, with a move towards companies which are more entrepreneurial in character.

The entrepreneur is the driving force behind the creation of the entrepreneurial enterprise. We define the entrepreneurial enterprise as one that is driven by the pursuit of market opportunity and is adept at identifying and capitalising on opportunities. The entrepreneurial enterprise is characterised by a closeness to customers and markets, the encouragement of innovations, risk-taking and flexibility. The essence of the entrepreneurial enterprise and the factors which shape its development should therefore be of interest to all of those concerned with developing companies, of all sizes, in a period of rapid change.

Change is the constant companion of the modern company. Change – driven by increasingly sophisticated customers, rapid advances in new technologies and increasing aspirations of workforces – is taking place at an accelerating rate in today's business environment. The major driver of change in any company must be market-related. Increased customer demands for choice, value and reliability offer opportunities for the development of new markets and niches. Those companies which are able to exploit these opportunities will require organisational structures based upon the needs of the customers they serve, rather than structures which evolve due to internal considerations.

Such organisations are not static but are able to experiment and adjust in response to changing markets and customer requirements. Flexibility and responsiveness are the new prerequisites for successful organisations. Systematic innovation has to become the new driving force behind companies. Peter Drucker defined innovation as consisting of purposeful and organised searches for changes. He called for innovation and entrepreneurial approaches to management if companies are to survive and prosper in a period of change.

There is a growing body of opinion that much traditional management theory is inadequate in the fast-changing conditions in which companies must now survive. It has been suggested that traditional methods work best in those activities where management can reasonably determine the expected results and by which methods they can be achieved. Fast-changing conditions mean that such situations occur less frequently in most companies.

The prerequisites of flexibility, responsiveness and innovation suggest the need for an organisational type which can thrive in an environment of constant change and is able to capitalise on the opportunities it offers. We believe that such a situation is the natural habitat of the entrepreneurial company. In our view the entrepreneurial enterprise, moulded by entrepreneurial thinking and characterised by entrepreneurial behaviour, is the most relevant model for organisational design as we move towards the next century.

What are the characteristics which make entrepreneurial companies different and which differentiate them from other organisations?

Entrepreneurial behaviour can manifest itself in a number of different ways. The Leith Agency, a small emerging advertising agency, has reacted to market demands for a wider range of services by creatively restructuring and setting up spin-out companies to add services while retaining creativity. Applied Sweepers, a manufacturer of road sweepers, has identified and capitalised on a niche market in an industry dominated by major manufacturers, through flexibility in design and innovative marketing approaches. One Devonshire Gardens, the Egon Ronay hotel of the year in 1993, has been able to thrive in a

15

period of recession in an industry with considerable overcapacity, due the identification of a niche opportunity and the provision of non-standard service.

Entrepreneurial activity therefore can show itself in a number of ways, from creative restructuring to niche dominance and from differentiated products to innovative strategies. These examples suggest that entrepreneurial companies create something different with regard to their products or services or the way that they implement their strategies. The ability to act in an innovative way, underpinned by a closeness to customers and markets, and a structure geared to flexibility and responsiveness are the hallmarks of the successful entrepreneurial company.

Although there are a number of indicators of entrepreneurial behaviour, there is one characteristic which is shared by all successful entrepreneurial companies and that is the thinking process which is inherent in the managers of such companies. Our experience of working with entrepreneurs leaves us in no doubt that entrepreneurship involves a quite distinct thinking process.

Show any group of people a situation and the entrepreneur among them is already identifying where the opportunities are and how they can be exploited. The genuine entrepreneur appears to be switched on to identifying and capitalising on opportunities. In successful entrepreneurial companies the leadership have enabled other people to act in an enterprising manner which has encouraged innovation at all levels and given the business an inherent flexibility. This can only happen when there is a shift in attitudes and thinking processes are more entrepreneurial.

This brings us to a number of fallacies about entrepreneurial companies:

- All small companies are entrepreneurial.
- All entrepreneur-led companies are entrepreneurial.
- Entrepreneurs are born not made.
- As companies increase their size then entrepreneurship must diminish.

16

As this book develops we shall examine these fallacies and dispel the myths which lie behind them. Entrepreneurial companies are not about size, nor exclusively about the type of person leading them, but rather they are about an attitude of mind – a thinking process which is apparent throughout the company.

In our opinion there are few genuine entrepreneurial companies – companies which are dynamic, flexible, switched on to market opportunities and able to manage change on an ongoing basis. In many companies entrepreneurial activity appears to plateau and even diminish after an initial period of growth. Also, many large companies find it difficult to change their cultures towards becoming more entrepreneurial.

If it is generally recognised that entrepreneurial behaviour should be encouraged, why do companies have difficulty in developing and maintaining such behaviour? We believe that the main reason is a lack of understanding about the development of entrepreneurial companies, a lack of knowledge about the essence of entrepreneurial behaviour and how this can be sustained over a period of time.

As companies develop, much of their activities is focused on developing systems and procedures to professionalise the business. Although this is necessary to allow control of an increasingly complex organisation, there is a danger that equal attention is not given to ensuring the business retains the enterprising characteristics which made it successful in the first place. There is a natural tension between remaining enterprising and professionalising that must be balanced and managed if the business is to develop and retain a sufficient level of entrepreneurial activity. One of the main reasons why larger organisations find it difficult to stimulate entrepreneurial behaviour is that they have many systems procedures and controls in place but the same effort is not put into developing people to act in an enterprising manner and creating a structure and culture which supports such behaviour.

Balancing Paradoxes in the Virgin Group

Feeling stifled by the demands of the City and his own shareholders, Branson bought Virgin back, added some partners and evolved a new way of running the business, almost a hybrid of two cultures. Using the financial disciplines of a public company, underpinned by the speed of action and entrepreneurial drive more commonly associated with a private company, he has built the Virgin Group into a billion-pound operation. His method of running it, once revolutionary, is now accepted as sound business practice

Sunday Times, May 1993

The starting point for the development of the entrepreneurial company has to be an examination of the attitudes and style of management. The leaders of any enterprise are the dominant influences on the direction it takes and the way it carries out its business. In the smaller, growing business, the leaders' attitudes to risk-taking, opportunity development and their inspirational qualities will have been the major driving forces in creating the business, and these skills and attitudes will continue to be important as the company moves forward. The leader must ensure that these attitudes are sustained and encouraged in others within the company. In larger organisations the management must re-examine their attitudes to innovation and ask whether they may be blockages to creating a more entrepreneurial business.

If entrepreneurial behaviour is to continue then the attitudes and behaviours of the people within the company will have to reflect this. Entrepreneurial behaviour does not come naturally for most people and there is therefore a need to nurture and cultivate such entrepreneurial attitudes throughout the organisation. We should not be striving to create a number of mini entrepreneurs as this is unrealistic, but rather to assist people to behave in a more enterprising manner: to be comfortable in a changing situation and to identify opportunities and initiate actions to improve the performance of the company.

For entrepreneurial behaviour to be effective over a period of time there is a need for a structure and culture that supports risk-taking, proactive behaviour and innovation. Organisational design needs to be based on customer requirements and offer the flexibility to create and respond to changes in the external environment. However, there is a danger that total flexibility leads to chaos. The structure of entrepreneurial enterprises needs to be flexible at the same time as providing enough stability to ensure discipline and continuity. Only by focusing on these key areas can we build genuine entrepreneurial companies. Such companies could be described in the following terms:

- The leadership is consciously building the policies and practices of entrepreneurial behaviour into the business.

- There is a management culture in which entrepreneurial behaviour is so deeply valued that it drives people's thinking and actions.

- Enterprising behaviour at all levels within the company is recognised as being the appropriate solution to achieving long-term objectives.

- There is close contact with customers and markets to provide the feedback and information necessary for innovation and enterprise.

- There are flexible, customer-focused structures which enhance and sustain entrepreneurial behaviour.

- Ongoing change is embraced as a natural part of everyday business.

19

If we are to create companies which can capitalise on the many opportunities that are presenting themselves in virtually every market place, then we must build organisations which are based on the above characteristics. This will require a significant shift in the attitudes of top management and the adoption of a range of practices which will allow them to create and sustain more entrepreneurial companies; companies which are driven by the pursuit of market opportunities and are adept at capitalising on such opportunities. In such companies entrepreneurial behaviour will offer scope for genuine competitive advantage in fast changing markets.

This book has been written for those who are interested in the development of entrepreneurial companies. It will examine how entrepreneurs develop and how the essence of entrepreneurship can be built into companies through the development of the above areas. It has been written from the perspective of the growing entrepreneurial company but will also offer an insight for individuals who are considering entrepreneurial start-ups and larger companies that are trying to increase the level of enterprising behaviour.

Part 2

Entrepreneurs: The Driving Force

Chapter 2

The Shape of the Entrepreneur

Populist Views

If there was a *Guinness Book of Records* award for the word with the biggest number of connotations, a strong contender would have to be "Entrepreneur". From the very start commentators (usually economists) put forward differing values and roles for this new social hybrid.

J. S. Mill, one of the first to utilise the name, considered direction, supervision, control and risk-taking to be the main functions of the entrepreneur. Adam Smith, generally considered to be a supporter of the free market values, classified the characteristics of the entrepreneur in terse terms: "the natural greed and rapacity of the entrepreneur".

The ambivalence which was present then persists in contemporary Britain. Thatcherism (leaning heavily on the Adam Smith Institute) pushed the view of individualism – not collectivism – as a valuable credo. The eighties did create entrepreneurs yet even during that period the popular connotations of entrepreneur were decidedly negative. Such views continue today. The cover story in the 28 May 1994 edition of the *Economist* questioned: "How does Britain View Its Entrepreneurs?" From research carried out by MORI it appeared that "only 32 per cent of Britons think entrepreneurs contribute a great deal to society (the same figure for plumbers)". The *Economist*'s view was particularly stark.

"Fawning over businessmen is no more sensible than worshipping politicians, pop stars or soccer players. Yet Britons are too cynical. America's computer industry can boast more businessmen acclaimed as heroes than the entire British economy."

In a similar vein Scottish Enterprise carried out a significant piece of research into the company birth rate statistics for Scotland. As well as discovering that Scotland's birth rate for new firms during the 80s was below the UK average, it also uncovered the popular views of the worth of entrepreneurs and again these were not so positive as in other countries surveyed, e.g. Germany and USA.

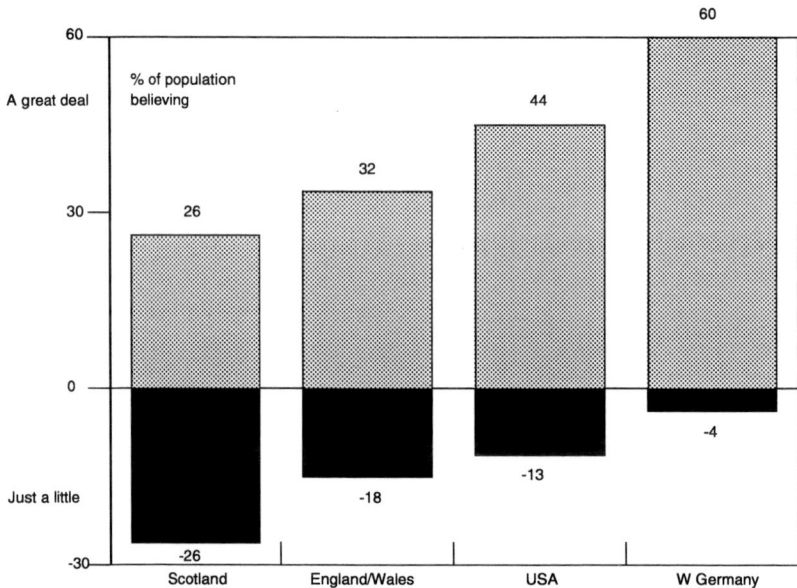

Perceptions: Entrepreneurs' Contribution to Society
(Source: Mori Survey)

The research went further into attitudes. One of the questions invited respondents to agree that entrepreneurs do care about other people. In Germany more than 50 per cent agreed, in America nearly 70 per cent. In Scotland the figure was 9 per cent. All respondents were asked to rank entrepreneurs amongst seven other occupations. In Germany they came second behind teachers, in England and Wales third (just behind bankers) but in Scotland they came fifth – behind manual workers.

Promoting an entrepreneurial culture is now viewed as an essential part of Scottish Enterprise's endeavours in reversing the trends in Scotland. However, in Scotland as in the rest of the UK, there is a set of preconceived notions about entrepreneurs which may take some shifting. They can be categorised as the following:

- **The entrepreneur as tycoon.** This connotation has the following characteristics: beyond the reach of most people, running an empire, large hand-rolled Havana cigars, light blue Rolls Royces, swimming pools in the back garden, second home in Marbella (at least), owning a Caribbean island (at best) and buccaneering in behaviour. Characters most likely to be associated with this view include Tiny Rowland, Berlusconi and Sir James Goldsmith.

- **The entrepreneur as shady dealer.** Enter stage left, Mr Arthur Daley, one notch up from a market-stall dealer with some dodgy equipment and a fast getaway. The shady dealer is morally moribund, with few or no loyalties beyond the immediate deal, who will sell anything to get a turn. Currently seen around the periphery of football clubs and their transfer moves. Also located in the popular imagination as a used car salesman.

- **The entrepreneur as gambler.** A close cousin of shady dealer. This entrepreneurial type is perceived as possibly affecting all levels of business person – gambling is endemic in this connotation. It shows itself at the top (share dealing, usually as an insider) to the bottom (minimal personal equity with maximum borrowings and marginal security). Likely to go bust with a trail of debt, most of which is to local suppliers.

- **The entrepreneur as inventor.** Ever since the demise of Clive Sinclair's operations we have the popular connotation that inventor entrepreneurs are barmy. Their judgement is so unsound as to be dangerous and in the face of the decline of British manufacturing they represent the comic irony of our failure to make and sell our way out.

These connotations represent the amount of baggage to be handled. Popular views will take some time to shift.

Entrepreneur's Views

Over a year we asked entrepreneurs (i.e. people who have started their own enterprise) if they saw themselves as "entrepreneurs". We asked this question of individuals who started and are running multi-million pound ventures, people whose companies are now industry leaders, people who have mid-sized companies and people who have started and are running small businesses. This runs to around 100 people and over 85 per cent do not see themselves as entrepreneurs! In their minds (both male and female) there is a generally held view that "entrepreneur" has now replaced "tycoon" in everyday parlance. This connotation is not always viewed as positive. It is little surprise that so few business creators align themselves with the word "entrepreneur".

The Paradox of "Entrepreneur"

If few business creators see themselves as "entrepreneurs" – perhaps due to negative connotations – the picture becomes more confusing when one tries to define their characteristics.

Soon after being asked if they see themselves as entrepreneurs they were asked: "What are the characteristics of entrepreneurs?" This question was asked of all the groupings, i.e. ranging from the demonstrably highly successful entrepreneurs through to early start-ups. There was a core of characteristics which recurred time and again. These were seen as:

- Self-confident
- Risk-taking
- Problem-solving
- Dedicated
- Positive-thinking
- Independent
- Opportunity-seeking.

Most, if not all, these characteristics were viewed as positive. Indeed, they are strong characteristics which many found attractive and admirable.

Therefore the paradox is that the perception of the word "entrepreneur" is not something which the majority of people who create businesses associate with, and yet, in their views, entrepreneurs possess a set of characteristics which most business creators recognise and align themselves to. These values – i.e. those which are seen as attractive, desirable, admirable – are sometimes recognised by the wider world and seen as heroic.

The Entrepreneur as Hero

If one turns to US culture one finds a clear admiration for the entrepreneur (highlighted in Scottish Enterprise's survey). There is a close connection between the entrepreneur and the pioneering individualist who encapsulates the American dream. *Fortune* magazine (the very title would be unacceptable in the UK) continually provides insight into the remarkable personal stories behind business success. This gets filtered through to the UK, yet we are aware that their culture praises the victory of the individualist who takes on the big guys and wins – such as Sam Walton (Wal-Mart) versus Sears or Bill Gates (Microsoft) versus IBM. The phenomenal rise of SUN Micros – started by four guys in sneakers and sweatshirts – is another example. At the most gross is the recognition of naked ambition enshrined in Trump Tower.

The entrepreneur as hero has a number of positive connotations in this realm – little man made big, iconoclast, the rags-to-riches process, pioneer, wealth creator and benefactor. As with many cultural values, these views do not transfer easily from the US to the UK. However, there are some indications that there are strong and positive connotations of the entrepreneur as hero.

The more flamboyant, or at least media-conscious, of entrepreneurs do seem to attract more column-inches, more air space and more sound bites than the corporate leaders of sturdy plc's. Richard Branson, Anita Roddick, Tom Farmer and the like are given the same treatment as entertainers or sports stars. Their activities outside of the basics of business are reported on and personality pieces are created for articles, not just in the business sections of newspapers but in lifestyle pages and glossy magazines. Such powerful individuals are recognised as "characters" and our interest in them is broad-ranging.

The business magazine *Scottish Business Insider* produces its annual review of the top people in Scottish business – the corporate elite. Recently it asked the top women in corporate Scotland who they most admired in business. The top ten of these most admired people were:

- Richard Branson
- Ann Gloag
- Anita Roddick
- John Harvey-Jones
- Tom Farmer
- Lord MacFarlane
- David Murray
- Pat Grant

Noticeably, seven out of the above eight are entrepreneurs rather than corporate executives.

Above all other considerations these entrepreneurial characters are perceived to run their companies. The stamp of their personalities is perceived to be on their businesses. Indeed, it is perceived that the businesses are indeed theirs whether the share base shows them as majority shareholder or not.

Such perceptions and admired qualities give these entrepreneurs a special form of leadership status. Their own leadership styles may vary considerably but we almost expect that they are proprietorial in their attitude (for good or ill). Stories of their management exploits which show this proprietorial approach are many. One straight from the horse's mouth is Tom Farmer's tale (oft repeated) of how he continually pays surprise visits to depots of Kwik-Fit. He happily tells you of the depot manager's surprise when Tom drops by for "a wee chat"! In behaving this way Tom Farmer and others like him are maintaining the identity of the leader and keeping their personalities felt in the company.

The entrepreneur as hero is, in UK terms, essentially about seeing entrepreneurs as larger than life leaders, as personalities and characters who create a style of doing business. We do not possess an entrepreneurial or enterprise culture similar to the US, where the social impact of wealth creation and job creation are readily acknowledged. Perhaps we should not aspire to have the entrepreneur as hero. However, we do need, and probably want, entrepreneurs as role models.

With all the various connotations of the characteristics of the entrepreneur it would be difficult to get a populist view of the essential qualities of the entrepreneur. The next section looks to academic research and commentary to give an insight into the essence of the entrepreneur.

The Essential Character of the Entrepreneur

Much research and academic debate takes place on the question as to whether entrepreneurs are born or made. However, our primary consideration is to describe the distinctive aspects of entrepreneurial behaviour which mark it apart. There is such a range of entrepreneurial behaviour that trying to define all entrepreneurs as the same is patently illogical. A prosaic view of what all entrepreneurs do is possible – such as "one who creates a business venture and fulfils a market opportunity".

Clearly such definitions shed little light on the motivations and the shaping influences which direct the behaviour of those we call entrepreneurs. In attempting to answer these questions we can begin to understand the implications for the main purpose of this book – i.e. how best can those who start businesses develop them into entrepreneurial companies.

In the past ten years or so there has been an increase in the number of academics engaged in the study of the entrepreneur as a discrete area of research. This is now showing itself in the professorial appointments and the gradual increase of entrepreneurial studies as part of undergraduate and in some cases postgraduate teaching. It is now feasible to talk about research in terms of a body of opinion which naturally has academic dissension. The nature/nurture debate and the ramifications for government policy continue to fuel much of the research.

As informed practitioners we take due cognisance of the various contributions made from academia and temper them with our own active research and experience.

The Need to Achieve

The major contribution to this area of the psychology of the entrepreneur has been the work of Douglas McLelland. His view is that people who score highly on the need to achieve (Nach) possess the following characteristics:

- Prefer personal responsibility for decisions
- Are moderate risk-takers as a function of skill
- Possess interest in concrete knowledge of the results of decisions (i.e. money as a measure of success).

He concludes that a need for achievement drives people to become entrepreneurs. This is largely borne out when one examines the successful entrepreneur. However, it could also be viewed that the need

30

for achievement is present in people who are successful in non-entrepreneurial activities and various research studies have emphasised this.

The Need for Independence

Time and time again research has recorded that people have stressed the need for independence as a very high motivational force. In our research findings it is almost top of the list every time. The description of this motivation is expressed in terms such as "to control my own destiny", "to do something for myself", "to be my own boss". Ivor Tiefenbrun, founder of Linn Products (the hi-fi manufacturers), has a quirky but essential similar view: "I wanted to decide for myself what time I got out of bed in the morning."

Some academics have gone to great lengths in analysing this motivation and there is a school of thought which has developed a Freudian view of this desire. In short, the thesis is that the entrepreneur feels thwarted by his employer (often a large corporation) who represents a bad father figure and that the act of creating a company represents the connection with an accepting mother or female figure which allows the entrepreneur the psychological freedom from the threatening demands of the authoritarian father influence. This is an extreme interpretation of the desire to break free.

Less extreme but coming from the same area is the view that the entrepreneur portrays a "cultural dissonance in being an individualist who suffers from an inability to fit in".

The above views present this motivation in negative terms. A more positive expression would be a desire to march to one's own tune and to take full responsibility for one's future.

Locus of Control

Closely related to the desire to achieve and for independence is the notion that one is master of one's destiny or at least there will be a high correlation between one's actions and the expected outcomes. The concept was first developed by J. B. Rotler and his categorisation of "locus of control" is defined as follows:

"When a reinforcement is perceived by the subject as following some action of his own but not being entirely contingent on his action, then in our culture, it is typically perceived as the result of luck, chance fate, as under the control of others, or as unpredictable because of the great complexity of the world. In these individuals we have labelled this as a belief in 'external control'. If the person perceives that the event is contingent upon his own behaviour or his own relatively permanent characteristics, we have termed this a belief in 'internal control'."

Subsequent research in various universities in the US has indicated that this belief in the internal locus of control results in more active efforts to affect positively the results of the venture rather than attributing less than desirable occurrences to being the result of luck or beyond the control of the entrepreneur.

Some research has also highlighted that the notion of internal locus of control is found in successful managers. This would tend towards the notion that it is a trait belonging to the successful and not exclusively the preserve of the entrepreneurial type. Therefore this concept may be a variable factor in gauging the extent of success and not an exclusive preserve of all entrepreneurs.

Adventuresome (Risk-taking)

Many people who have created businesses express a view that they are not gamblers or risk-takers. This is often sharply contrasted with the views of others both in seeing the entrepreneur as a risk-taker and that their actions consequently involve a high degree of risk management. This perspective is strengthened by the view that to fail in business is an irredeemable sin. With such a cultural shibboleth it isn't surprising that many people are literally scared off from ever starting a business as the "risks" seem too high.

Our view is that there is no absolute measurement of risk. All risk is relative and a large slice of that risk is perception. If one accepts that the entrepreneurial type scores high on the need to achieve and has a higher than average sense of locus of control then it is a straightforward connection between these and a high self-belief. Self-belief and internal locus of control combine to increase the expectancy of success and consequently the reduction in the perception of risk. Therefore risk is a perception which is checked or cancelled by the prospect of success. For the entrepreneurial type the perception of risk/reward is clearly positive. Their view of the future is therefore generally optimistic and they perceive challenges rather than risks.

There is a strong body of research and opinion which focuses on these four traits – need for achievement, need for independence, locus of control and attitudes to risk. This tends to present a view that entrepreneurs are born not made.

We certainly think that there are very early shaping influences which contribute to the likelihood of being entrepreneurial, the most important being a sense of self-belief and a belief that one is somehow different or special. In the many discussions we have had with entrepreneurs we find various examples which indicate that early social influences help greatly in inculcating a sense of self-belief.

One of the most remarkable triggers for such self-belief was described for us by Jim Faulds, founder of Faulds Advertising – now Scotland's biggest advertising agency. He precisely states that the sense of self-belief to do something out of the ordinary was "on 25 May 1967 at 5.40 pm in Lisbon". Jim was a young teenager then and his favourite team, Glasgow Celtic, filled with ordinary people led by the (extra)ordinary Jock Stein and supported by ordinary people, in winning the European Cup had scaled the heights which no British club had previously reached. For him the lesson was simple – it was possible to do something extraordinary from an ordinary background.

To translate this into entrepreneurial activity needs action. This happens later in the adult formation when people learn from the behaviour of others and copy those actions. Early influences will shape the possibility of being entrepreneurial but the biggest contribution comes from experiences in early adulthood.

Many studies have taken a comparative approach, presenting an archetype of the entrepreneurial character with the opposite being administrative or non-innovative. In our view too much has been made of this forced dichotomy. A more accurate assessment of the "traits" approach to the definition of the entrepreneur is that there exists a range of personality traits. John Burch's view of entrepreneurial activity in his book *Entrepreneurship* presents a neat illustration of such traits. He presents the view that there is continuum of entrepreneurial types:

- Copycat entrepreneur
- Opportunistic entrepreneur
- Venture capitalist
- Innovative entrepreneur
- Inventrepreneur.

This presents an interesting notion that there are specific classifications or types of entrepreneur. However, one could argue that the inventrepreneur is not the purest form of entrepreneur nor are we sure that venture capitalist necessarily fits the bill. However, it introduces the idea that there are gradations of entrepreneur.

Our view is that it is more valuable to think in terms of gradations of behaviour which entrepreneurial types will exhibit. In making observations about entrepreneurial and non-entrepreneurial behaviour we believe from our experience that there is one major area of behaviour which is unambiguously different. It is the area of judgement.

Opportunistic Judgement

Decision-making reveals the way in which people see opportunity, evaluate strategy and commit resources. There is in our experience a distinctive entrepreneurial way of making such evaluations in contrast to its antithesis – the administrative way. These "judgements" can be illustrated thus:

	Entrepreneurial	Corporatist
Strategic Orientation	Pursuit of opportunities	Exploitation of already controlled resources
Opportunity Identification	Ongoing, intuitive	Structured search
Opportunity Capitalisation	Speed and action orientation	Cautious advancement

Strategic Orientation. The genuine entrepreneur sees change as necessary and is always looking for opportunities or new ways of doing things. A strategic orientation, in thought and in action, towards exploiting opportunities, as opposed to husbanding existing resources, is the hallmark of the entrepreneur. This search for innovation – whether proactive or reactive, consciously or unconsciously – sets the entrepreneur apart from the managerial type.

Many successful entrepreneurs are also very good at intuitive strategic thinking. According to Ohmae, strategic thinking involves a mixture of analysis and creativity which is applied to create advantage for the company vis à vis the competition. This "mental elasticity" is the hallmark of a true strategic thinker. Although many entrepreneurs do not have formal training in business strategy, the successful ones display this mental elasticity by intuitively gathering and processing information about the external environment and the potential opportunity in a way which allows them to create advantage in the market place.

Opportunity Identification. The genuine entrepreneur is an individual who can spot an opportunity and is attracted to it like a magnet. He has a sort of "entrepreneurial antenna" which is always switched on and tuned in to changes and situations as they present themselves. This involves a fair degree of lateral thinking to spot niches which would be ignored or passed over by more conventional thinkers, as well as a strong self-belief in their intuitive ability to spot winning ideas. This of course can be a major weakness as well as a strength.

Opportunity Capitalisation. There are many individuals with good ideas but the successful entrepreneur is one who can identify and evaluate an opportunity before quickly moving to the implementation stage. This is where many of the entrepreneurial characteristics show themselves. Action orientation, an ability to bend the rules and take short cuts, and a single-minded focus on achieving a vision all separate the entrepreneur from the more cautious and slower-moving manager. The challenge of achieving the vision is a major driving force behind the success of entrepreneurs and it is this focus which gives the entrepreneur the impetus to succeed where many others may fail.

The entrepreneurial "mindset" is the major factor which differentiates entrepreneurial behaviour from other types. A mindset is a description of the way that we make sense of our experiences. How often do we become interested in a new car or fashion and then notice the same model or style almost everywhere we look? This is because our mindset is triggered to see things which previously would have passed unnoticed.

Many entrepreneurs have opportunity-based mindsets which have a strong influence on their perception of events. They spot opportunities because they have a mindset which is focused on seeing gaps, differences and patterns.

Vision and Purpose

A person's mindset can be shaped by a number of factors. This is backed up by research which shows that entrepreneurs come from different backgrounds and all walks of life. The unifying factor for this diverse group is the thought processes which they bring to any situation. Entrepreneurs think differently from other people and this is what distinguishes them from the masses.

> The entrepreneurial perspective starts with a picture of a well defined future, and then comes back to the present with the intention of changing it to match the vision.

Fortune magazine did a profile on America's best young entrepreneurs – those who were under forty and had created multi-million dollar companies. The profiles showed a collection of individuals who had been able to think differently, to pursue a vision and to cope with massive change on an ongoing basis. One entrepreneur explained his success as being able to cope with change, being speedy, unconventional and relentlessly creative in discerning what new services people might need. All of the entrepreneurs pushed forward the idea that to make it big you have to be different and pursue a radical vision.

As well as thinking differently successful entrepreneurs also are goal-oriented. Achievement is a major driving force for entrepreneurs. From day one of their enterprise many successful entrepreneurs have a clear vision of what they want to achieve. The challenge of achieving this vision is a major driving force behind the success of new ventures and it is this focus which gives the entrepreneur the impetus to succeed where many others may fail. In our opinion it is this mix of entrepreneurial thinking and the drive to achieve their goals which characterises successful entrepreneurs and makes them such an important force in the creation of dynamic companies.

The driving force of vision provides the catalyst for the actions of the entrepreneur. There is a psychological compulsion to close the gap between the vision of the future and the current position of the entrepreneur. The compulsion of the vision does not belong therefore to some rational thought process. Indeed, one could easily be persuaded that the whole activity of creating businesses is non-rational.

Visioning has been classified as a right-brain activity, similar to that involved in music and the arts. Its effect is motivational and perhaps inspirational (at the very least to the founders of the business!). It can occur in the like minds of a few people but by the laws of human nature it is unlikely to be engendered by committee. Perhaps that is why there are so many dull and uninspiring mission statements hung on the walls of corporations around the globe.

One of the best descriptions of the effect of vision is the following from Tom Watson, IBM's founder:

> IBM is what it is today for three special reasons. The first reason is that, at the very beginning, I had a very clear picture of what the company would look like when it was finally done. You might say I had a model in my mind of what it would look like when the dream - my vision - was in place.
>
> The second reason is that once I had that picture, I then asked myself how a company which looked like that would have to act. I then created a picture of how IBM would act when it was finally done.
>
> The third reason IBM has been so successful was that once I had a picture of how IBM would look when the dream was in place and how such a company would have to act, I then realised that, unless we began to act that way from the very beginning, we would never get there. In other words, I realised that for IBM to become a great company it would have to act like a great company long before it ever became one.
>
> From the outset, IBM was fashioned after the template of my vision. And each and every day we attempted to model the company after that template. At the end of each day, we asked ourselves how well we did, discovered the disparity between where we were and where we had committed ourselves to be, and, at the start of the following day, set out to make up for the difference.
>
> Every day at IBM was a day devoted to business development, not doing business. We didn't do business at IBM, we built one.
>
> *Tom Watson, Founder of IBM*

Such a compelling vision propels the entrepreneur and motivates others to follow. The degree of the strength of vision is of course variable across those who create businesses. In our view it is the supreme trait of the entrepreneurial type. The trait is one which appears at different stages in one's life and for this reason tends to belie the notion that entrepreneurs are born rather than made.

The Innovation Factors

It is not difficult to put forward the view that innovation is central to entrepreneurial behaviour. Schumpeter, one of the first to write on the subject, felt that it was the central characteristic of entrepreneurial endeavour. Others have subsequently linked this to the realm of psychology in stressing that the entrepreneur possesses a distinctive approach to "problem-solving" which revels in creating innovative solutions.

Yet one cannot help but notice that there is innovation as "problem-solving" in many walks of life and there are probably just as many opportunities in large corporations as in the entrepreneur's firm. In our view there is a further key definition of "innovation". Business innovation can only be defined in terms of the marketplace. Innovation is not synonymous with invention.

Market-Led Innovation

The most successful of all business strategies have market-based innovation at their core and the realities demonstrate that those who are first into a market stand the greatest chance of dominating in the longer term. We would stress the need to underline innovation as innovation in the marketplace. Innovation can so easily be viewed as invention which, while close, is not the same thing. Being innovative could be in the way the product is sold rather than in creating a truly new product.

A case in point would be the phenomenally successful Direct Line,

The Royal Bank of Scotland's insurance "product". This is not a new product as the consumer still receives a conventional insurance policy. The innovation was in the selling and utilising the power of information technology as an enabler. Peter Wood, the entrepreneur who created Direct Line, has been well rewarded for this most innovative of "inventions".

By contrast, Clive Sinclair's C5 recumbent bicycle was the clearest example of "invention" rather than "innovation". This had nothing to do with perceiving a market-based opportunity for innovation and a lot to do with creation for its own sake.

Less dramatically, virtually all businesses start-ups require a degree of innovation. How many founders would describe their products or services as "me too"? However, the desire in many people to be different or differentiated can tip the balance away from market-based innovation. We have come across scores of business plans which contained such intricate differentiation that it becomes hard to see where the value lies for the purchaser. It may be different but where is the market demand?

The entrepreneurial skill is in perceiving the effective balance between differentiation and an obvious market need. Even the best can get this wrong. A few years ago David Murray, of Murray International Holdings and Rangers Football Club, backed a team of experienced news people to create a new Scottish Sunday tabloid. One could see how this could be quite different from the existing *Post* and *Mail*. A number of factors contributed to its short life and demise. However, in hindsight the question begs as to whether there was the market demand for a third Scottish Sunday tabloid when there were two entrenched leaders already in place.

Innovation and Creating Businesses

A more clearly defined form of innovation rests with those individuals who have the ability to repeatedly create businesses which are innovative in market terms. Innovation does not always mean creating a market but recognising the shifts within marketplaces which give scope for a new business to be born.

The most media proclaimed example of an entrepreneur who is able to innovate time and time again is Richard Branson. Many of his businesses show very clear examples – Virgin Records (innovation in independent production), Virgin Mega Stores (innovation in music retailing), Virgin Airlines (innovation in airline passenger service), etc. It is reported that there is a policy within the Virgin Group to have companies of fifty employees. When any company becomes bigger than this there begins the process of creating a new company to allow the sense of ownership which fosters a dynamic and innovatory approach. Branson's approach has had notable success with the launch of new companies in evidence, such as Virgin AM, Virgin Cola and Virgin Vodka.

At the other end of the scale one can regularly find unsuccessful entrepreneurs who are constantly chasing the latest thing and missing out. In the words of Sir James Goldsmith: "If you see a bandwagon – it's too late." The ability to be regularly innovative is a hard act to master and calls for great judgement and timing.

Being innovative, however many times, also calls upon the entrepreneur and his team to be very effective in managing the new as opposed to managing the routine. Once again there are surely gradations in this which one can see and even measure.

The Wealth Factors

Much of what is written about entrepreneurs appears to ignore or understate attitudes towards wealth. Perhaps this is due to our cultural distaste of ostentatious wealth and a subsequent reticence of business creators to speak openly about financial success. Once again we believe there are specific gradations of entrepreneurs which are in this case governed by their attitude towards wealth.

At the outset of many a business venture there are uncertainties which only a fool would discount. Many business people say that at that point they had little thought of specific material gain from the venture. Therefore attitudes to wealth may be something which develops over time. Whether this is the case or whether attitudes are defined earlier, we have noted four gradations:

1. Those for whom business creation is a domestic or hobby pursuit and who in fact may take a cut in "salary" for the satisfaction of business creation.
2. Those who view business creation as a means of improving their personal income stream.
3. Those who are seriously interested in wealth creation – for riches, for power, for the access it may bring or for the scope to do good works.
4. Those who see finance as a marker of business success – almost to the extent of having little intrinsic worth.

Attitudes to wealth have a powerful influence upon the size of the business the entrepreneur wishes to create. This may not be so apparent in the infancy of the business but certainly becomes a factor beyond the three-year watershed.

What Type of Entrepreneur?

The essential character of the entrepreneur has therefore a rich variety of factors – namely:

• The need to achieve
• The need for independence
• Locus of control within the self
• Adventurous
• Market-focused innovation
• Opportunistic judgement
• Vision and purpose
• Wealth orientation.

All of these will be present to a greater or lesser degree. The extent to which they are present and the mix of them will determine the likely level and the nature of entrepreneurial actions. This in itself will not predict the levels of success individual entrepreneurs will have. Serendipity, luck and an understanding bank manager also have their part to play!

These factors coalesce into three broad descriptions of entrepreneurial type:

- The single-venture entrepreneur
- The growth entrepreneur
- The serial entrepreneur.

The Single-Venture Entrepreneur

This describes the vast majority of people who start a business. The wealth orientation is most likely to be concerned largely with improving a revenue stream, the extent of innovation is low and the psychological imperatives are satisfied at an early stage. A number of businesses demonstrate these features, such as those which are carried out from home, family businesses which provide family members with a job and a salary and a host of businesses which are broadly described as "lifestyle" businesses.

The Growth Entrepreneur

Here the wealth orientation is more concerned with building capital value as well as improving a revenue stream. The company will be innovative within a narrow band of business activities and the psychological imperatives will contain higher doses of vision and need to achieve.

The scope for growth will of course be shaped by a range of market factors and therefore one can find a range of business sizes in this category. The desire for growth is focused on a unitary business or on a small collection of linked businesses. Very often these business activities will stem from a particular skill which the entrepreneur has (e.g. building) or from managerial experience in a specific industrial sector. The antecedents will therefore be closely related to the entrepreneur's experiences.

The Serial Entrepreneur

Here the wealth orientation will be high or be regarded as a marker for "success". The degree of business innovation will manifest itself in regular mould-breaking activities. The psychological imperatives will contain large measures of risk-taking propensities and the successful serial entrepreneur will have a broad vision which is not self-limiting. The serial entrepreneur who is successful over time will see himself more and more in the role of the entrepreneur rather than identifying with the business activities he may have started. The numbers of such entrepreneurs are small and may in some measure be justifiably seen as the "classic" entrepreneurial type.

At one end of the spectrum one can identify the serial entrepreneur with the tycoon. The tycoon is seen buying and selling businesses as commodities. At the other end of the spectrum we find the more modest activity of starting a number of businesses which are not necessarily related, or starting a business, selling it and starting again.

For the serial entrepreneur who goes on to create very substantial businesses there appears to be a limitless level of ambition. Whether that ambition is fuelled by a desire to acquire more and more wealth, by a narcissistic desire to self-promote, by a simple joy in creating and building businesses or by lofty ideals, these entrepreneurs all exude energy. Tom Farmer, one of Scotland's best, highlights this factor as one of the most important reasons for his success. In simple terms it translates into a capacity for work which can leave many of us feeling positively slothful.

One may conclude that the serial entrepreneur is the most classically entrepreneurial. However, we are not suggesting that this necessarily predicts success. Picking winners from a set of characteristics is notoriously difficult as many a worthy piece of academic research has found out.

The concern of this book is to examine the factors which, given fair circumstance, are more important for success. The next chapter considers the personal characteristics which become more important for those who are going beyond the "lifestyle" type of business into growth phases.

Chapter 3

The Entrepreneur and the Growing Business

As any business grows there are increasing requirements for change: an increasingly competitive situation, the development of new opportunities and additional resources, all require a shift in the breadth and depth of management within the business. The pivotal role of the entrepreneur suggests that these changes must be driven and managed by the entrepreneur and this is likely to require significant personal change if the business is to move forward. The skills and behaviours which were necessary to establish the business need to be modified and augmented if the business is to grow. In order to implement the changes that will be required, the entrepreneur needs to be aware of the key issues surrounding the growth and development of the business and understand the implications of these for their own development.

Every business goes through an establishment phase where it has to tackle the issues of start-up, which involve conceiving the initial business idea and establishing it within its market. During this phase of development the main issues are establishing a customer base, generating a positive cash flow and setting up the basic controls necessary to conduct business. This stage is about proving there is a business and it is where the entrepreneur's drive and energy can be critical in turning the nascent idea into a viable business. The key maxims at this stage could be seen as:

- Get bigger
- Get paid
- Get on.

The successful entrepreneurial company is able to develop through this first phase due to the driving force of the entrepreneur, who has built strengths through detailed customer knowledge, a focus on niche markets, short lines of communication, flexibility and adaptability. The entrepreneur is the major driver of the business in this phase and will revel in an environment which is relatively unstructured and allows the freedom for direct action and a hands-on approach.

If the start-up phase is successfully negotiated then the business achieves a degree of stability where it has created a customer base, can support the owners financially and is returning a profit. When the business reaches a stage where it is "established" the owners are faced with a number of critical development issues and choices. These issues require fundamental decisions about the entrepreneur's aspirations, the strategic development of the business and how to keep the company entrepreneurial.

For established companies there are key decisions to be made about the future development. This involves the owner(s) of the company examining their vision and clarifying what their future aspirations are. Many entrepreneurs reach a comfort level at some stage – a point where they have achieved many of their initial aspirations. This places inhibitions and constraints on future development. We have already described this as a lack of entrepreneurial drive and it leads to a situation where companies plateau at what we would call early maturity, where in-built constraints from the owner inhibit the business from really testing or achieving its growth potential.

Other, more entrepreneurial companies use the initial establishment of the business as a launch pad towards rapid growth and development.

In such companies there is the recognition that it is necessary to capitalise on existing opportunities and constantly to be searching for new ones. For some companies this is just a natural progression of their original vision but for others there is a key decision point or catalyst – usually around the aspirations of the owner(s) – which spurs the future development.

Gibb in his work with growing companies at Durham Business School has identified a number of broad characterisations of growth companies: from *Early growth companies*, which develop from start up to a £1-2 million turnover over a three to four-year period, to *Super growth start-up companies*, which go from £1 million to £10 million plus over a ten-year period. Undoubtedly one of the major differences between these categories of company is the drive and aspirations of the owners.

The early growth phase is critical in the development of the entrepreneurial company. It is during this phase that many of the attitudes and norms are formed. This is a time of considerable internal change within the company and one of the most significant of these changes is with regard to the entrepreneur and how the business is managed.

The Tensions of Growth

As the business grows, a number of potential conflicts of focus and allocation of resources arise in the areas of leadership, management, structure and strategy. These potential conflicts give rise to a series of tensions which must be managed. We have described flexibility as being one of the key characteristics of the growth entrepreneur and this ability is tested to the full in the management of potentially conflicting pulls on resources which occur in managing the tensions brought about by growth.

Tension of leadership

In the early stages of the growth of the entrepreneurial company there is normally a dynamic, action-oriented style of leadership which motivates others and enables the development of the business. The personal (and financial) commitment of the entrepreneur to the business idea and the drive to succeed mean that in most cases the management style tends towards directive. The close interaction between entrepreneurs and employees and the entrepreneur's involvement in the day-to-day operations of the company means that this leadership style can be highly effective in developing the business.

However, as we shall discuss later in this chapter, the successful growth of the business is dependent upon the entrepreneur stepping back from day-to-day operations and a greater contribution from a senior management team. This will be achieved only if there is a move towards a more consultative and participative management style. The entrepreneur has to develop a style which will allow the maximum contribution from other managers, while retaining the dynamic style which has been instrumental in building the business and will be necessary to drive the business towards new opportunities.

Tension in Strategy

Earlier we described successful entrepreneurs as being effective intuitive strategic thinkers, by being able to gather and process information about market opportunities in a way that allows them to create an advantage in the market place. However, as any company grows there will be a need to increase the level of strategic planning – to undertake more rigorous analysis and have a greater clarity of the rationale and criteria for strategic decision-making.

There are a number of reasons for this:

- Increasing complexity of the business
- Increasing competitive pressure
- Managers need to be exposed to the strategic process
- The need for regular strategic reviews.

49

Increasing the level of strategic planning should not be at the expense of the ability to be opportunistic, as this is the essence of the entrepreneurial company and will continue to be a key strength as the business grows. By planning we mean a conscious effort to increase the level of strategic awareness and strategic thinking through a clear focus or vision, understanding clearly the area competitive advantage, a strong awareness of changes in customers' needs and developing clear parameters against which opportunities can be screened. In this way increasing the strategic planning ability will not slow down the speed of decision-making or decrease the flexibility of the company, but rather provide greater strategic awareness which will help the business to remain entrepreneurial.

Tension in structure

Flexibility is one of the major strengths of the growing company and therefore there is a need to develop a structure which allows for changes from the existing situation in response to, or in anticipation of, market changes. However, total flexibility makes it difficult for any organisation to retain any continuity. This suggests some need for a degree of stability.

The constant reorganisation which takes place within the growing company means that there is the need for stability to provide for continuity and identity, while developing the capability for flexibility and rapid change. This calls for a structure which can combine these two characteristics.

Tensions in Management

Growth and development bring an increased scale and complexity to the business and this calls for increasing management skills throughout the company. The professionalising of the management, through development of the skills of the existing managers or bringing in new management, is a key step in ensuring growth is managed. Professional management and the skills and thinking processes which are required to be effective in this area can be, as we discussed in the previous chapter, quite different from the thinking processes and attributes of the entrepreneur.

Professionalising the management may bring difficulties in that it may develop individuals who are effective at controlling what is already there and do not display an inclination towards innovation or the pursuit of new opportunities. We must ensure that the natural tension between enterprising and professionalising is maintained by keeping a focus on creating enterprising managers.

Managing these tensions may seem daunting but, as Charles Handy writes, the paradoxes facing the modern manager do not have to be resolved – only managed. What these tensions show is that if the entrepreneur is to manage the growth of the business successfully he has to recognise the dynamics of growth brought about by the tensions and the potential paradoxes within them. Successful growth will take place only where the entrepreneur is constantly aware of the dynamics of the situation and how these relate to the key issues facing the business.

Lessons from examples of high-growth companies have shown that there is a need for a flexibility in management thinking which is related to learning, modification and ongoing improvement. There is a danger that a focus on implementing standards and systems can impose a rigidity in the thinking processes which may inhibit the dynamic thinking that is required to successfully manage growth and remain entrepreneurial.

The ability to manage the tensions of growth and increase the professionalisation of the business, while at the same time retaining its entrepreneurial character, is the key to managing the growth of the entrepreneurial company.

The Entrepreneur as Manager

In many situations the entrepreneur is one of the major barriers to the company remaining entrepreneurial as it develops. The personality traits which are a positive stimulus to starting a business can act as barriers to the entrepreneur developing the company past a certain stage.

A major problem for the entrepreneur occurs because of the increasing requirement for management within the business. The growing numbers of people and overall shift in the scale of the business mean there is a requirement for a greater level of management skills to control and develop the company. We have already highlighted the differences between the thinking processes of entrepreneurs and managers and therefore we should not be surprised that many entrepreneurs find it difficult to adjust to an increasingly managerial role.

Increasing the level of management skills is critical for any growing company since one of the major contributors to the success, or otherwise, of any company is the quality of management within it. This can involve developing those who are there and/or bringing in new management. These managers need to be managed. As the business grows the entrepreneur must become more involved in managing. The hands-on approach of the entrepreneur means that he finds it difficult to give up control and gets increasingly bogged down in the operational aspects of the business. This can have the effect of blunting the entrepreneurial skills which had been critical in creating and establishing the business.

Many entrepreneurs do not make good managers. The problem is that effective management requires the ability to be less hands-on, more team-focused and calls for considerable interpersonal skills to develop and motivate others. In our work with entrepreneurs and growing companies we asked employees about their views of the entrepreneur as a manager. From a list of fifty key managerial attributes the following table describes the most commonly identified development areas:

Key Managerial Weaknesses for Entrepreneurs

1   Do not keep people informed

2   Do not give regular feedback to people

3   Are not effective delegators

4   Do not bring out the best in people

5   Do not spend time developing people

6   Do not accept criticism well

Source: Matrix

The typical perception of entrepreneurs by their subordinates is of individuals who are poor delegators and do not spend enough time in the areas of internal communication or people development. There is also a lack of sensitivity as characterised in not showing consideration for the needs of others, lack of flexibility and not accepting criticism. This can lead to poor people management and interpersonal clashes. These characteristics suggest that many entrepreneurs are not very good at getting the best out of the people they employ.

Our experience suggests that many entrepreneurs are uncomfortable with key aspects of the managerial role. Roberts, in his studies into entrepreneurs in American high-technology companies, describes Founder's Disease: "The inability of the founding entrepreneurs to develop their managerial and leadership capacity as rapidly as the firm's size and future potential growth".

Entrepreneurs can also have problems with regard to their leadership style. Because entrepreneurs drive new ideas, with sometimes only their vision and belief in themselves to sustain them, it should come as no surprise that their managerial approach tends towards the autocratic. Effective managers, however, recognise that a more democratic approach is more sensible for practical and motivational reasons, as well as the need to develop the capabilities of other individuals.

Entrepreneurs can find it difficult to move towards a more participative approach.

Entrepreneurs who are unable to make personal changes and resolve the conflict over their role as the business grows, can become a major constraining influence on the growth of the business. In some situations, where there are strong external shareholders, the entrepreneur may come under increasing pressure to step down and be replaced by someone who has the requisite skills for the growth stage of the company. One example was the founding managing director of a nursing home company whose position was "terminated". According to the chairman this was a question of management styles as the existing MD was replaced by a professional manager who could practise a more participative style.

It is relatively rare for one individual to have the skills necessary to excel as a manager and as an entrepreneur. Indeed, there is a danger of the entrepreneur concentrating on the development of his management skills at the expense of the entrepreneurial nous which has been the main factor in building the business. The entrepreneur must work at developing his managerial and leadership skills but strike the correct balance with retaining his entrepreneurial flair.

The difficulties of being an effective entrepreneurial manager mean that if the business is to be successful then the founder entrepreneur must recognise the requirement for a change in his role. The founding entrepreneur's attitudes towards risk-taking and opportunity development, and his inspirational ability, will have been the major driving forces in getting the company to where it is, and these skills and attitudes will be crucial in the company's future development. He must find a way of utilising these skills while ensuring that effective management skills are also built into the business.

Self-Development for the Entrepreneur of the Growing Company

Much of what follows by way of recommendation has come from our experiences with our director development programme, "Breakthrough

Management". This programme is specifically for directors of small companies who have the desire to grow their enterprises to a medium-sized operations. The programme addresses that transition and provides helpful techniques which will enable the leader to grow and develop the company in the most beneficial fashion.

Much of the focus of the programme is on the development of the entrepreneurial leader. We see the main factors of personal development as:

- Creating vision, purpose and goals
- Role development
- Strategic thinking.

In each of these areas there are challenges for most entrepreneurs. The challenges are put forward not as a good way to manage but as the fundamental factors which have a strong bearing on whether the company can become bigger, brighter and better. Having run the programme for some five or six years, we have had more than 200 directors participate. Looking back on the growth and development of their businesses, many of them testify to the importance of these factors in the changes within themselves as leaders.

Vision, Purpose and Goals

As we described previously, one of the most important facets of the success of the classic entrepreneur is their strength of purpose, vision and commitment to goals; these three things coalesce into a drive and a force which can often pull the company through difficult or demanding circumstances. They coalesce but there are different aspects to the three elements.

- **Vision** combines the ability to perceive trends and opportunities with the creative imagination to see a specific result. It is fuelled not only by perceptions of the conditions but also by the dreams of ambition.

- **Purpose** is the commitment to an ideal or to values; these can be seen in the business realm in such things as quality, customer service, technical brilliance, etc. For example, where one finds a small business whose service is outstanding one will usually find a zealot to that ideal at the helm.

- **Goals** are generally more prosaic and are usually expressed in terms of growth in turnover, return on sales, position in the industry or some such figure. Of great importance is both the existence of well held goals and the steady determination to turn these into development actions. These actions in turn need to be achieved step by step.

The essential challenge in vision, purpose and goals is to keep them fresh, meaningful and personally stimulating. Without their vibrant existence the company will go to sleep and in the most extreme of circumstances slip into a coma. For many a person who has started and developed a venture there comes a time when the vision thing dims and the personal desire may wane. The reasons for this can be that the personal fulfilment has occurred – the sense of personal achievement therefore holds little motivation. Perhaps the desire for personal acquisition has also plateaued. These situations may halt the progress of the company but they may also be breakthrough points.

To avoid such a plateau, it is desirable that the vision for the company does not have too many limitations. Many of the more successful growth entrepreneurs describe their ambitions for the company in terms such as "to realise the full potential of the business". This kind of view emphasises that there is no pre-set limitations on the development of the business. As a fundamental attitude this is helpful but it is hardly inspiring for oneself or for others. To recreate vision and purpose the entrepreneur needs to be inspired by the shape of the future.

A most helpful way of recreating inspiration is to look at other companies as "role models". The high rollers like Richard Branson and Anita Roddick are regularly cited as people whom we admire as entrepreneurs. There is a strong interest in the personality of such people and there are an increasing numbers of books, videos and TV programmes which allow us to see what makes them tick. Without doubt they can be inspiring and perhaps they can truly be seen as role models.

A more specific way of recreating a purposeful vision is to seek out companies which are in the next stage of development and mirror their behaviour. Seeing things from a different perspective is also helpful and travelling to foreign countries to see other businesses is often a source of inspiration. In so doing one is also overcoming the loneliness of the managing director. This in itself is highly important in preventing an introverted view which can develop within the small company.

One of the major successes of our "Breakthrough Management" programme has been the sharing of experiences amongst group of MDs. Another recent development in this vein has been to visit other growth companies in the USA and continental Europe. This has been both inspiring and educational. In most cases the leaders of the growth companies have developed models for the growth of the business. These are not theoretical models but real models based on other companies and perspectives from other MDs. The models then give one a series of goals to aim at, a clarity of purpose and hopefully a recreated vision.

Role Development

A fundamental aspect of personal development is the change in role of the leader of the company. We describe this change in the growing company as moving away from operational roles to developmental roles. The entrepreneur who wants the business to grow will move away from his own initial comfort zone, the area which he knows best. Perhaps this is making the product or selling the product – in some cases it is doing the whole thing, from checking the raw material to doing the cash book. These operational roles must be replaced by developmental ones. They are to do with changing the company, leading others, developing the strategy of the company and perhaps in the process getting back some of the energy that characterised the start-up period.

Underpinning this change is the development of those around the leader or leaders which will allow this to happen. Another key aspect of this is the ability of the leader to manage himself – in terms of time, resources and delegation.

To help in this one can review one's time in terms of work level analysis. This consists of creating five bands of work level from the most mundane and routine to the developmental:

Work Level Analysis	
5	• Leading change in the company • Developing key people • Searching out new opportunities • Formulating strategy
4	• Setting goals • Plans • Policies • Guidelines • Reviewing allocation of resources
3	• Instigating action • Monitoring achievement
2	• Operational problem-solving
1	• Routine operational tasks
Level	**Activity**

Source: Matrix; Breakthrough Management

For the progressive-minded MD the changes should be to increase the amount of effective time spent in levels 4 and 5. To gain further insight into one's performance requires a time log to be taken over a standard week or fortnight. This can then be analysed in terms of work level and with goals set to shift the proportions of time spent. Stopping going to the bank every week, checking invoices or wasting time with the mail may seem unexciting changes but collectively they provide the leader with a significant opportunity to spend time on the growth and development of the business. Not uncommonly we find that there can be a gain of around 20 per cent by delegating such tasks or by more effective use of time.

The process is not necessarily an overnight success but it can be fundamental to the development of the business. Participants on the "Breakthrough" programme have often said that this has been the most important development for their companies. Two of our participants said that they felt a bit uncomfortable having time on their hands as they had been successful in carrying out such changes. Their companies had doubled in size over the two or three years since being on the programme, from £2 million to £4 million and from £3 million to £6 million. They attributed much of that to their own ability to change roles.

Having found this bonus of time, how should one fill it? The developmental roles fall into the following characteristics:

- Coaching
- Driving change
- Championing entrepreneurial development.

Coaching others means that the leader will spend time encouraging the performance of other people within the company. Quite often in the growing company this will be the development of a tier of management beneath the directors of the company. Their development will fall into two broad categories: helping professionalise the company or helping the enterprising development of the business. Later in this section we give examples of how these come into action.

59

The skills required for effective coaching are clearly people development skills. These may be present in entrepreneurial types but there may also be tension between the energy to make things happen and the patience required for the development of others.

As the business grows there is an increasing need to have an effective management team that can combine the individual managers' knowledge and abilities to tackle increasingly complex decisions and situations. This places new demands upon the existing managers as their role develops and responsibilities increase. The management within the company need to develop their attitudes and capabilities in the following areas:

- Ability to cope with ambiguity
- Increased commercial skills
- Enhanced strategic thinking
- Improved interpersonal skills
- Greater autonomy and initiative
- Ability to learn and develop.

Driving change is to do with making the growing company focus on the real issues that will bring success. The changes will be central to the strategy of the company and therefore are to do with competitive advantage. The change issues will be likely to concern such things as quality management, service values, product innovation, cost-effectiveness, etc. The role of the leader in this is to unite the company around a common set of principles, creating simplicity in operation, providing clarity on performance management and giving the lead in campaigns to improve circumstances.

Championing entrepreneurial development is more complex and is the central concern of this book. In terms of the development of the leader's role there should be an evaluation of how much time to be spent in developing more customers, entering new markets and launching new products. As we shall expand on later, there are benefits and shortcomings if the leader chooses to spend too much time in this aspect of the role.

Attitudes and Behaviours of the Entrepreneur

We have already discussed the difficulties entrepreneurs face as the business grows – moving from operational to developmental, the need to move from doing to delegating, and the need to involve others. Although there are a number of blockages which constrain attitudinal and behavioural change in entrepreneurs these must be overcome to move towards the following:

- Increase in consultative/participative management
- Real delegation of tasks and decisions
- Greater use of the senior management team
- Increasing trust in other managers
- More effective two-way communication.

These factors can be combined in the following diagram:

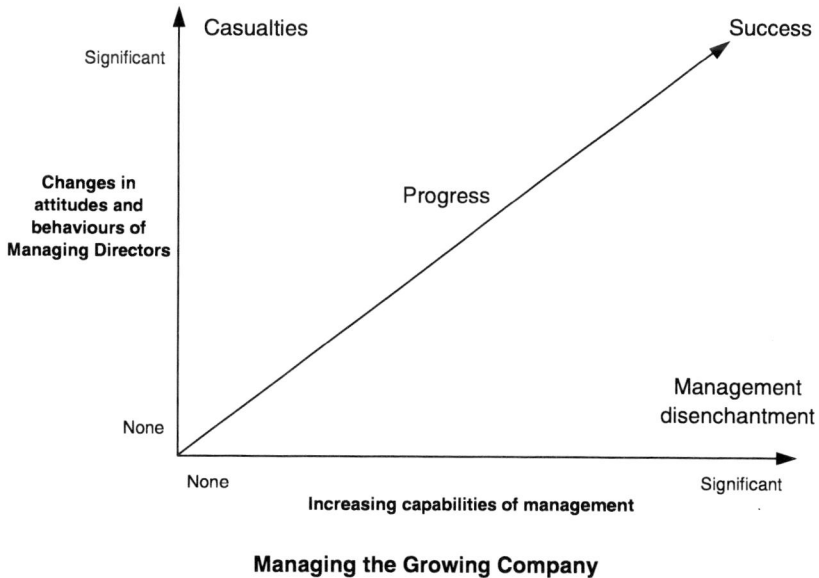

Managing the Growing Company

The diagram suggests that the growth of entrepreneurial companies will not be managed effectively unless there is significant change in the attitudes and behaviours of the founding entrepreneur and in the attitudes and capabilities of the other management in the company. This statement may seem obvious but while all growing entrepreneurial companies would aspire towards "success", the practicalities of making it happen are more complex.

At the heart of such changes lies a classic entrepreneur's dilemma: the entrepreneur must be prepared to give the management more freedom and involve them more in real decision-making, or else the management will lack the motivation to develop their capabilities and seek responsibility and autonomy. However, the entrepreneur may not be willing to give greater responsibility to the management because he perceives that they lack initiative and capability.

If such thought processes prevail within the company then it will be locked into attitudes which inhibit growth, with no change in the entrepreneur's behaviour and no stimulus for the management to develop their capabilities. In this situation the entrepreneur is locked into the negative self-fulfilling prophecy of "I cannot change because I lack the trust in others' capabilities to change". From this position companies will find it impossible to develop and progress.

Our diagram also suggests that change is necessary in both the entrepreneur and the manager and therefore such development must take place in tandem. However, an escape from the "entrepreneur's dilemma" requires positive action and leadership of the change by the entrepreneur. This means that a significant change in attitudes and behaviour must come from the entrepreneur in the first instance and it is only by showing such a lead that he will start to create an environment within which the management are motivated towards increasing responsibility and autonomy, and begin to behave in a more enterprising manner.

A lack of trust by the entrepreneur in his senior management, either because of a perceived lack of capabilities or a need to keep control of the business, is a major debilitating factor in the growth of any company. This can lead to resentment, frustration and demotivation within the senior management team – a situation of management disenchantment where the managers are making efforts to develop and are being frustrated by the entrepreneur. This can be particularly frustrating for new management who have been brought into the company for their skills in key areas, and it is not unusual for these managers to seek new opportunities in other companies where they perceive that their talents and abilities can be better utilised.

The top left of the diagram describes the situation where the entrepreneur has recognised the need for changes and has made significant efforts to change his attitudes and develop his capabilities but has not seen the same changes in the management. Although this situation may occur in the short term – where the entrepreneur has taken the lead by making personal changes and is developing the enterprising and managerial skills of the management team – it cannot be maintained in the longer term, and if there is no evidence of the managers' capabilities and attitudes improving then their positions need to be closely examined and further changes in the senior team may be required.

If the entrepreneur is to change then he must face up to the issues we have outlined and recognise that genuine change will require a rethink in his attitudes and a discipline towards making change happen. A clearer understanding of the entrepreneur's role in a growing company is necessary if the business is to develop. Only by reviewing and modifying their approach can entrepreneurs ensure that their style and attitudes are not inhibiting the development of the business and that their role allows them to capitalise on their entrepreneurial strengths.

Strategic Thinking

There is a tension between the need for some formality in strategic planning within the growing company and the natural opportunism of the entrepreneurial company. The need for flexibility and responsiveness in companies of all sizes is now leading to some debate on the value of such planning. Most vociferous in condemning formal strategic planning is Henry Mintzberg, the Canadian management guru. In his book *The Rise and Fall of Strategic Planning* he damns the rigidity of planning and puts other virtues in place:

"To be superbly successful you have had to be a visionary – someone with a very novel view of the world and a real sense of where you are going. If you have that you can get away with the commercial equivalent of murder. Many of the great strategies are simply great visions. They can be more effective than the most carefully constructed plan."

Mintzberg's targets are the large corporations and the MBA "factories" which produce, in his terms, "trivial strategists". Once again the practices of large organisations are being questioned and solutions are being offered which seem to belong to the smaller enterprise.

In our experience of the smaller company, there is scope for visionary thinking linked to strong strategic perspectives. In essence it is demonstrated in successful start-ups. For a successful start-up there has been a good understanding of the competitive environment, a clarity about the way to find and keep customers and enough attention paid to differentiation for the venture to find its feet and have early success.

As the company develops there can be a diminution of that early clarity of vision and strategy. If the leader of the company becomes more and more concerned with its internal operation there is a good chance that the strategic perspective can be diminished. To counter that there is the need, as we have already said, to change the role of the leader. There is also a benefit in terms of increasing the amount of quality information which can be used for strategic decision-making. In our work with growing companies we have devised a way of looking at this issue and helping entrepreneurs improve the information levels in the company. This approach is based on levels of information which correspond to the growth of the company, with both the internal performance of the company and the external marketplace in which it operates. It can be graphically represented as follows:

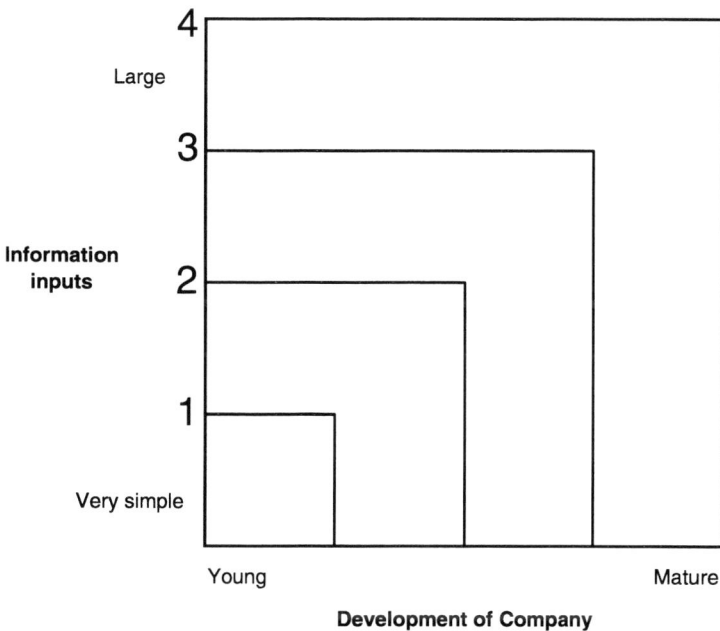

Development of Company

This graphic representation has four thresholds; each represents a constraint based on information for management control and strategic choice.

- **Threshold 1** is information sufficient for basic business controls.
- **Threshold 2** is information regarding internal company performance and external sales performance.
- **Threshold 3** is information required for strategic decision-making, competitor activity, product positioning – for example, the strategic triangle (see page 142).
- **Threshold 4** is information gathered on diverse market opportunities and product opportunities.

The specific content of the information at each level is as follows:

THRESHOLD 1	THRESHOLD 2

1. Cash flow information
 	
2. Control of working capital
 	
3. Sales records
 	
4. Basic production scheduling
 	
5. Regular management accounting information.
	1. Manufacturing or processing performance
	   • work standards
	   • productivity
	   • quality costs
	   • accurate cost information
	
	2. Sales performance
	   • product performance
	   • sales personnel performance
	   • efficiency of marketing
	
	3. Information for budgetary control.

THRESHOLD 3	**THRESHOLD 4**

1. Market Information
   • geographic split
   • rate of new entrants
   • threat of substitutes
   • power of suppliers
   • power of buyers
   • market share
   • market segments
   • trends
   • industry norms
 	
2. Customers
   • performance figures
   • rate of growth
   • key competitive pressure for them
   • buying process analysis
   • their industry norms
   • their perceptions of you
 	
3. Competitors
   • market share
   • their performance figures
   • who their customers are
   • benefits of their products and services
   • their strengths and weaknesses
	Systematic approach to generation of strategic information, plus the review and updating of such information on an ongoing basis. Such a level of information requires a significant investment of resources in this function.

Source: Matrix; Breakthrough Management

As can be seen, there is a definite shift between levels 2 and 3 and a marked change in emphasis from level 3 to 4. These changes indicate an increasing need to introduce a degree of systematic gathering of information which for many entrepreneurs is often resisted as it can be viewed as a diminution of the reliance on pure "gut feel".

If the leader is able to introduce a degree of rigour into gathering information, spend a reasonable mount of time thinking strategically and focus on being a well differentiated niche player then the company stands a good chance of long-term development. Strategic thinking in these terms is not the same as formal strategic planning. For the entrepreneurial company operating in the fashion described above it is "gut feel" at a sublime level.

For the majority of growth entrepreneurs strategic thinking should be concerned chiefly with the primary competitive issues of differentiation and niche effectiveness. Even if one is extremely fortunate in creating a mass-market product there will most likely be the need to differentiate it strongly in order to achieve market share. In doing so, niche marketing may well be a suitable tactic (see page 131).

Developing Strategic Thinking

Many entrepreneurs are good intuitive strategic thinkers and are adept at spotting opportunities and capitalising on them. However, the ability to think strategically is a skill which must be continually honed. As the business grows there is a need for greater strategic awareness as the business situation becomes more complex.

At start-up the strategic decisions involve finding ways of getting into the market and becoming established. As the business grows the entrepreneurial company has to make judgements about the significance of increasing competitive pressure, changes in market dynamics and new trends and opportunities, as well as being able to the evaluate new opportunities in the context of these changes and the existing business situation.

Successful growth entrepreneurs build on their intuitive strategic decision-making ability to sharpen strategic thinking and become better at building businesses. This involves:

- Understanding and updating information about the key strategic issues facing the business.
- Knowing the company's strategic position and being aware of the impact changes in the environment may have on this.
- Having a set of criteria against which new opportunities can be evaluated.
- Having a clearly defined growth strategy.

By increasing the levels of strategic awareness the company will enhance its capability to be flexible and opportunistic, in that strategic decisions can be made faster and with greater confidence that they are correct.

One of the key issues in increasing strategic awareness is to develop the level of strategic thinking within the company. Kenichi Ohmae, in his book *The Mind of the Strategist,* states that: "Successful business strategies result not from rigorous analysis but from a particular state of mind." Ohmae is not suggesting that analysis is unimportant but rather that the overall thinking processes and attitudes are more important. In order to improve strategic thinking skills we need to be aware of the key issues involved.

- **Analysis is the starting point.** The true strategic thinker understands that analysis is required to allow the dissection and sifting of information to identify the pertinent issues and stimulate the creative process.

- **Strike a balance between analysis and creativity.** Strategic thinking requires a balance between right and left brain thinking. Analysis without creativity can lead to a flawed approach to strategy and vice versa. Ohmae talks about the "mental elasticity" which is the hallmark of the strategic thinker.

- **Strive for the complete picture.** Any strategy is only as good as the level of information which supports it. While it is impossible to have perfect information in any situation, striving for as much of the complete picture as it is possible, or cost-effective, to achieve will improve the quality of strategic decision-making.

- **The importance of timing.** Even the most well thought out strategy can be doomed to failure before it is implemented if it is not timed to fit in with changes in the market and environment.

- **Strategic thinking as a daily discipline.** If the business strategy is to be effective then it must shape the daily decision-making within the business. The entrepreneur must be aware of the impact of actions on business strategy. This effectively means being aware of each action and thought process – is it moving your company towards a fulfilment of strategic choice or responding to events? The daily discipline of strategic thinking has honed many successful companies into knowing what can be defined as a "business paradigm". More simply, those whose understanding of the strategic positioning of their company is highest are most likely to develop a formula for business success.

Part 3

Creating an Enterprising Culture

Chapter 4

Leading the Entrepreneurial Company

Having examined the nature of entrepreneurs and the issues they face in growing their businesses, we now consider the actions they must take to keep their businesses entrepreneurial. The first area is the leadership approach which the entrepreneur develops.

The importance of good leadership cannot be stressed too much. Without effective leadership at all levels within a company there will be poor teamwork, people not giving of their best, a lack of direction and ultimately the company not achieving its objectives. If one examines poorly performing organisations, those where the growth has plateaued or those which consistently fail to achieve their objectives, then in the majority of such cases the lack of performance can be traced back to the quality of the leadership. Many organisations lack leadership or, where it does exist, it is patchy, with a lack of a consistent quality of leadership throughout the company. Organisations which have a leadership vacuum can be characterised by:

- No sense of purpose
- People going through the motions
- Lack of priorities and urgency
- Missed deadlines
- Lack of teamwork.

Leadership is a critical factor in the performance of all types of organisation, but there are particular issues relating to the entrepreneurial company which suggest that the leadership approach takes on a specific significance. The key role of the entrepreneur in creating and developing the business means that he will exert considerable influence on the business and its values.

It has been suggested that in a small to medium-sized company the impact of the leader is like an oversized footprint whose shadow can cover everything. The drive for speed, flexibility and responsiveness and the short lines between the top and the bottom layers mean that entrepreneurial leaders are likely to have a strong direct influence on the actions of people at all levels within the organisation. Accordingly, entrepreneurial leaders may be much closer to the people within the company than in other, larger organisations. This requirement for close-up leadership means that the actions of the leader will have direct impact on people's performance.

The relative intimacy between entrepreneurial leaders and followers can bring with it major benefits for the business but it can also lead to specific problems. In the initial phases of the entrepreneurial company the entrepreneur's drive and focus can provide a dynamic approach to leadership which motivates others and encourages the development of the company. However, as the business grows the entrepreneur needs to examine this leadership style and question whether it is appropriate to take the company forward, or whether the approach to leadership makes the company overdependent on one individual whose style may be stifling people's capabilities and initiative.

There are many positive characteristics of entrepreneurs which can be utilised to provide effective leadership. The entrepreneur's drive, sense of purpose, determination and self-confidence can all be combined to provide a dynamic, charismatic approach to leading others. However, these traits can also make the entrepreneur impatient with others who do not act in a similar manner and can lead to difficulties in understanding or accepting other approaches or different points of view.

In the entrepreneurial company the example and attitudes of the entrepreneur are critical. Cameron McCall is a highly successful entrepreneur who has been involved in a number of businesses. He describes the importance of the entrepreneur as leader and suggests that there is "a certain culture which results from the way that you are".

Entrepreneurial Leadership and Purpose

The founding entrepreneur has a major role to play in instilling enterprising behaviour into the company. The entrepreneur needs to be aware of this and recognise the actions and behaviour he can use to develop and encourage enterprising behaviour throughout the organisation. As the founder and leader, the entrepreneur has a considerable influence on the people within the company who look to him for guidance and direction. As we have suggested, the founder is the major influence in setting the norms and culture of the company and therefore any move towards entrepreneurial values and behaviour will be influenced to a considerable degree by the leadership he displays.

A key aspect of leadership is the provision of guidance and inspiration to others within the business. In any high-performing team, whether in business or in sport, there are shared goals and a clarity of purpose. The importance of purpose and a shared sense of direction cannot be underestimated in any company. The sense of purpose should relate to the what the company is in business to achieve, as well as how it can be achieved. The sense of purpose should be as much about behaviour as it is about goals. "People look to entrepreneurs for inspiration, ideas and enthusiasm" is a view put forward by Gio Benedetti, a serial entrepreneur who has a track record in building successful companies.This view relates to the sense of purpose which entrepreneurs should be building into their companies.

A concept which is closely allied to purpose is vision. As we stated earlier, the driving force of a strong personal vision can provide the catalyst for the entrepreneur. This vision can also be developed as a way of getting other people within the business to share a common purpose.

In this way a clear vision, which other people can relate to, can be a positive catalyst for change within the company. The entrepreneur should be able to unite people toward a common goal and approach as this can be a powerful motivator. It can be used to provide a focus for effort within the business which allows everyone to pull together. People want clarity from their leaders and this can be achieved through a clear sense of purpose or vision.

Vision is the essence of what the company is about: what it is in business to achieve. A vision is more than a simple slogan or mission statement and has to be based on actions as well as words. Many attempts at creating a verbal statement of a company's vision have proven to be empty rhetoric, not recognising that a live vision is a complex mixture of aspirations, values and how the company does business.

In many situations mission statements and slogans only serve to create a focus for cynicism within the business. However, any company which can display evidence of a live, purposeful vision – shared by the key members of the business – will be a dynamic organisation with a clear focus on the way forward. The vision provides a focus for actions, pulls people together and acts as a powerful facilitator of change.

The reality of a live vision is that it is rarely about the big things – the grand actions as typified by company away-days, conferences or the annual "state of the nation" address. Although these are important in the overall process of leading the business, a live vision is about actions which take place on an ongoing basis and a number of small events – everyday communication of the key business messages, daily enthusiasm and the creation of empathy at all levels. As one entrepreneur articulated to us, "It is important to constantly share your view of the world with everyone else to help them think like you." If you are able to get even a handful of people thinking in the same way as you, then you are starting to create a vision which will form the basis for everyday actions within the business.

Within the entrepreneurial company there are three main issues surrounding need to use a shared vision as a basis for a leadership style which enthuses others:

- Developing the vision
- Communicating the vision
- Driving the vision.

Although we have suggested in previous chapters that strength of vision is an important driving force for an entrepreneur, it is our experience that many entrepreneurs do not capitalise on this strength to develop the company. In the entrepreneurial company the starting point for the development of the vision has to come from the owner/entrepreneur.

Many entrepreneurs have difficulty in sharing their own personal vision as it relates to individual achievement or personal wealth creation. A vision which assists in the process of enthusing people towards action will have to take account of the aspirations of others as well as the foresight and personal aspirations of the entrepreneur. Many entrepreneurs are uncomfortable with this as they believe that it will be difficult to match their personal vision with a corporate vision that others help shape. This may be a difficult concept but if you are able to create a group of like-minded people who are focused on a shared objective then you have created a powerful grouping to achieve that objective.

In some situations we have come across, entrepreneurs have lost sight of their original vision or find it increasingly difficult to find a challenge within the business. Work done by the Centre for Creative Leadership into the attitudes of entrepreneurs identified the continued need for self-motivation as a key issue. This fits in with our earlier assertion that entrepreneurial activity can plateau at varying times over the life of a business. In order to inspire others the leader has to be inspired himself.

A word which is often used by entrepreneurs in describing their motivations in building a business is "excitement". There is no doubt that the emerging company is an exciting environment to work in and the continual challenges can be a major motivator. Allan Galashan, of Applied Sweepers, keeps the entrepreneurial essence of his business by continually providing new challenges. He talks of "always looking to go the extra mile in finding avenues to develop and deploy our talents into". If the entrepreneur is no longer excited by the business or ambivalent about its future development, then this will be picked up very quickly by others within the company. Initially this can lead to a general feeling of lack of challenge and sense of purpose, and from this reducing levels of motivation can quickly follow. The entrepreneurial leader needs to keep people motivated by challenging what the company is doing, how it is doing it, and setting future targets and goals.

The Flexible Leader

Another key aspect of the entrepreneur as leader is the way they do things – the management style they embrace. Many entrepreneurs just want to get on with their business: developing the market opportunities and moving along at breakneck speed with little concern for the niceties of the appropriateness of leadership styles. However, as we have already suggested, this is a short-term view and is one of the main reasons why many companies which are led by entrepreneurs do not fulfil their potential.

The entrepreneur who is interested in building a long-term business which is capable of innovation and speed of response, recognises the importance of taking other people with him and harnessing their capabilities to the full. Most entrepreneurs would agree with the sentiments but find difficulty in the practical application of such an approach.

One of the main elements of providing a more appropriate leadership style is the ability to develop a flexible approach to leadership. This approach involves harnessing the positive aspects of the entrepreneur's natural leadership style while developing a more balanced approach to getting the most from others.

The essence of the flexible approach to leadership can be summarised by two continuums which describe key aspects of leadership behaviour:

FREEDOM ....CONTROL

LEADING ....FOLLOWING

Freedom and Control

In their management classic *In Search of Excellence*, Peters and Waterman identified the attributes of excellent companies. One of these was "Simultaneous loose/tight properties". This meant that excellent companies had a balance between the controls necessary to allow the monitoring and improvement of performance and the freedom and responsibility necessary to encourage individuals and groups to achieve maximum performance.

It is possible to develop a successful company where the focus is on tight controls. It is also possible to develop a successful company where a loose culture allows freedom of actions. Real excellence occurs where there are "simultaneous loose tight" properties.

In the same way we believe that excellent leaders should be striving to develop simultaneous loose/tight skills or, as in our continuum, balancing freedom and control. This involves allowing individuals the levels of responsibility necessary to encourage ownership and involvement while controlling key business decisions and the overall performance.

The major strength of the freedom/control continuum occurs when a leader is able to keep a balance between these apparently diverse traits. Leaders must be able to manage the tension between these areas and capitalise on the significant positive benefits which can be derived by keeping them in balance.

Where leaders choose to give people considerable freedom to carry out and complete tasks with the minimum supervision and "interference" they must recognise and ensure that their people understand that freedom cannot be given without responsibility. Freedom is a product of discipline and therefore freedom of action must be balanced by responsibility. If people are not disciplined there is a danger of situations slipping out of control. If, however, there are pre-set objectives then these can be monitored on an ongoing basis. With such controls in place a leader can confidently empower his people and give them considerable freedom in achieving these objectives. Where a leader is more comfortable with a tight or highly controlled approach then he has to be prepared to let go to get the maximum contribution from his people. Control cannot be seen to be suffocating and therefore must be tempered with flexibility.

Leading and Following

The other continuum we use to explain flexible leadership lies between Leading and Supporting. Supporting suggests that in order to motivate and get the maximum performance the entrepreneur will have to provide support to others. The entrepreneur will need to learn to lead from behind, or be a follower, in that he is facilitating and supporting others in the achievement of objectives. This will ensure that others will also take responsibility for making change happen within the company.

However, in order to introduce the concept of continuous improvement, to instil the urgency and requirements for major change and to encourage others to accept these ideas, the leader will also need to lead from the front in introducing and driving change. This approach to leadership therefore requires a careful balance between driving change and allowing others to take responsibility for their actions. The ability to get change started, focus people and gain commitment needs to be weighed up against the requirement to empower others through providing the support necessary to allow them to achieve their objectives. The balance between Leading and Following will change over time depending upon the situation and the individuals involved.

Many entrepreneurs are comfortable in the leading role as this is the approach they will have employed in building the business. The entrepreneur will tend to lead from the front – by example and through the development of "can do" attitudes within the business. This is a major strength of the entrepreneur and should not be inhibited if the business is to move forward. One of the main leadership roles of any entrepreneur should be to provide drive and energy and this defining role should continue.

The Supporting role, however, is about enabling and empowering a group of people to take responsibility and ownership of their actions and therefore requires skills in facilitation, coaching and in understanding the people dynamics of any situation. These are not areas where the skills of entrepreneurial types naturally lie and therefore it may be difficult for the entrepreneur to strike a balance between these approaches .

As with the Freedom/Control continuum there is a natural tension between Leading and Supporting. The key is identifying which approach is most appropriate at a given time. The relationship between these areas is dynamic, changing over time.

Flexible Leadership Model

Both of our continuums can be integrated into one model which shows us the key aspects of a flexible approach to leadership. The four areas are equally important and the successful leader has to develop skills in each of them. He has to be able to be a Leader and a Follower and he has to be able to provide Freedom and Control.

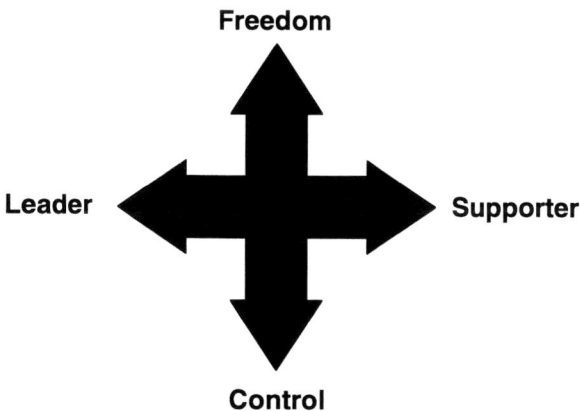

Freedom

Leader   **Supporter**

Control

As well as developing skills in these four areas and being able to strike a balance across the two continuums the entrepreneur has to be able to identify situations where one side of the continuum is more appropriate than the other and to react accordingly. This calls for a high degree of awareness about a particular situation and the flexibility to move to each end of the continuum when appropriate.

Many entrepreneurs will lack the flexibility to develop this approach to leadership and in practice we have come across few examples of entrepreneurs who have mastered such an approach (although there are many who are trying). It is interesting to note that many second-time entrepreneurs – those who are in the process of building their second business – are more aware of the mistakes they made the first time round and try to avoid them in their new venture. These entrepreneurs show an increased awareness of the importance of surrounding themselves with key people and providing a more supportive and less constraining approach to managing them.

Leadership signals

A key aspect of entrepreneurial leadership is the signals given by the entrepreneur. Leaders are constantly sending out signals to others within the company and these relate to how things are done as well as what is done. The leaders of any company are constantly promoting a set of values and behaviours through their actions and behaviour. The importance of the entrepreneur in driving the company and the close-up leadership style which they employ give their actions a particular significance.

Entrepreneurs have to recognise the importance of the signals they send out and be acutely aware of the implications and impact on others. The entrepreneur has the opportunity to set the tone or influence people's attitudes towards a particular way of thinking with a few well chosen actions.

Examples of these signals are:

- Public recognition of an employee who has found an innovative approach to doing something.
- Evangelising about the importance of ongoing improvement to every employee at every opportunity.
- Well-timed interventions to clamp down on unacceptable behaviours.
- Provision of resources to innovators.
- Time taken to seek out and provide recognition to individuals and groups at all levels within the company.
- Continually communicating about, and relating actions to, the main issues facing the company.

The actions of the leader give an indication of the behaviour which is valued and rewarded within the company. To consider their own performance in this respect, entrepreneurs need to reflect upon a number of questions:

- What signals are being sent to people within the company by your behaviour?
- What behaviour do you reward?
- What behaviour do you measure?
- Are you supporting and reinforcing enterprising behaviour?
- Is there a consistency between what you say and what you do?
- Are you sending out conflicting signals?
- Do people tell you what they think you want to hear?
- Does the business still excite you?

The entrepreneurial approach to leadership is a close-up management style which builds "can do" attitudes. This is achieved by example, recognition and a large number of ongoing actions. Regular signals to managers and employees about what is important and how business should be conducted, backed up by consistent actions by the leader, are the first steps in building an entrepreneurial company and stimulating enterprising behaviour from the people in the business. This may involve the creating and sharing of a vision; it certainly involves developing a sense of purpose, cultivating common beliefs and surrounding yourself with people who can relate to what the business is trying to achieve.

The Entrepreneur as Leader

Gio Benedetti, chairman of Benedetti Holdings, is a typical example of a serial entrepreneur. Benedetti started a small dry-cleaning business in the 1960s, expanded it into industrial clothing services and sold it to BET in 1990 for £13 million. He then became involved in Silcock Express, which was sold in 1993 for £52 million. He has now formed a holding company which specialises in buying firms which are in a poor trading position and developing them.

As you would expect, Benedetti has some clear views on how to build entrepreneurial companies. He stresses the competitive aspect of building a business and suggests that he doesn't build businesses, he fights battles. This is exemplified by his motto: "Kill the opposition." Benedetti believes that the key to building a competitive edge is through "selling differences". This requires an ongoing search for innovative ways of doing things - "if you stop innovating the business will go stale or bust"!

Benedetti believes that there are certain aspects of the entrepreneur's leadership role which are critical in building a successful company. He highlights the danger of the entrepreneur becoming buried in the detail of running the company as the business grows. He also recognises the need for entrepreneurs to surround themselves with managers who think in a more structured way, to complement the creativity of the entrepreneur.

His own approach to leadership is to look at everything with a visioning aspect, keeping the overall business as his perspective. He also believes that people look to him for inspiration, ideas and enthusiasm. He sees his main job as keeping the momentum going within the business by focusing his managers on the important issues and continually asking of them – "What did you do today to develop the business?"

Chapter 5

Developing Enterprising People

The previous chapters have examined the importance of the entrepreneur and the leadership style that he must cultivate to develop an entrepreneurial company. This is only part of the equation; the entrepreneur cannot hope to sustain an entrepreneurial company of any significant size through only his own efforts. The creation of a company which is truly entrepreneurial will require the support of other people – a management team and a workforce who are at ease with the concept and realities of being part of an entrepreneurial company.

We have already suggested that entrepreneurial behaviour does not come naturally for most people. We have also seen that entrepreneurs have a distinct thinking process which differentiates them from the majority of people. We need to recognise that not everyone has the drive, commitment and psychological make-up to be an entrepreneur, but most people have the potential to be more enterprising. Indeed, many entrepreneurs are uncomfortable with the concept of more than one entrepreneur in the company, believing that this is their role. An entrepreneurial company is not necessarily one that is populated by genuine entrepreneurs but rather one that is entrepreneurially focused – in which the fundamental motivators are towards the pursuit of opportunities – and organised in a way which allows it to identify and capitalise on such opportunities. This will only happen when the majority of the people in the company behave in an enterprising manner.

There is a distinction between entrepreneurial behaviour and enterprising behaviour and the initial focus in the entrepreneurial company should be towards getting people to be more enterprising. However, there is a case, at senior management level, for developing some managers towards behaviour which could rightly be described as entrepreneurial. This is because many of the market opportunities will happen only if there are a number of entrepreneurial people to drive and capitalise on them.

Enterprising behaviour is about being prepared to show initiative and take responsibility to undertake ventures or actions which could be seen as having an element of risk. As with entrepreneurial behaviour, there are two main elements of enterprising behaviour: opportunity identification and opportunity maximisation. Enterprising people are constantly looking for opportunities to improve the existing situation, either by modifying or improving the existing product/service or the processes which are required to produce the product/service. In this way enterprising behaviour can be internal or external to the company. Accordingly, enterprising behaviour is characterised by a high degree of upward innovation with fresh ideas being generated at all levels within the company.

Enterprising behaviour is also about getting things done – people being prepared to implement changes and take responsibility for their actions. In such a situation people seek autonomy for decision-making, have well developed analytical skills and can demonstrate a track record for getting the right things done – actions which ultimately lead to improvements in the performance of the business. It is this pragmatic link between thinking and doing which makes enterprising behaviour so valuable. If such behaviour is cultivated throughout the company it will give a competitive edge through speed of decision-making, innovation and flexibility.

Above all else, enterprising people are comfortable in a situation of ongoing change. They recognise the need for a company to be continually changing and thrive in a changing environment. Such people can only develop in a company which is enterprising and where innovation, risk-taking and flexibility are encouraged and developed.

Entrepreneurs would readily accept that this is the type of people they would want within their company. How then can we get people to behave in a more enterprising manner? We can start to answer this question by considering the nature of enterprising behaviour. Enterprising behaviour should not be seen as a one-off or a reaction to a particular situation but rather an ongoing way of thinking.

In order for enterprising behaviour to take hold within the company it should be the norm for people to act in this way, with a culture which provides support and encouragement by managers and peers. In a truly entrepreneurial company enterprising behaviour is something that takes place as a matter of course or routine.

At the start-up of any business most people within it have to act in an enterprising way. In this phase the urgency which is required to establish the business idea necessitates a need for continual innovative thinking, flexibility and a high commitment level from most of the employees. There is an obvious sense of purpose which stimulates and encourages enterprising behaviour.

As any business grows it becomes more difficult to retain the excitement of the start-up phase and it becomes more difficult to maintain the urgency and clarity of purpose. Communication can become fragmented, separate departments are established and it becomes increasingly difficult to align the various goals and objectives of individuals and groups. The entrepreneur needs to think carefully about how to retain the urgency and motivation at this stage.

Our experience is that there is one key differentiating area which sets the entrepreneurial company apart from others: the real test of an entrepreneurial company lies in the dominant thinking processes which prevail within the company. Entrepreneurial thinking and subsequent enterprising behaviour do not come naturally, and it requires considerable effort to develop them within any company. As we discussed in the previous chapter, the leaders have a key role in consciously building policies and practices of entrepreneurial behaviour into the company. The starting point in developing entrepreneurial people therefore lies in the actions of the leadership.

However, leadership alone will not create enterprising people. We need to consider other ways of developing enterprising behaviours and attitudes throughout the company. In most cases this is likely to require major rather than minor behaviour change and this will require development in its widest sense, with a focus on improving attitudes, skills and knowledge.

In order to get employees to act in an enterprising manner we need to understand what motivates their behaviour. Entrepreneurs act in a particular way because they are driven towards the pursuit of their objectives. It follows then that people are more likely to act in an enterprising manner if this leads them towards achieving their own ambitions. This calls for the creation of an environment which allows people to achieve their own goals and aspirations. If we do not understand what motivates employees and build in ways of allowing them to achieve their aspirations within the overall goals of the business, then it will be very difficult to stimulate enterprising behaviour. Genuine enterprising behaviour will take place only when people perceive the benefits and are intrinsically motivated and committed towards this way of behaving.

The starting point in cascading enterprising behaviour to all levels in the company is in the development of the next level of management. We earlier described the managerial mindset with words such as cautious, incremental, controlled and structured, which suggests that this group think in a totally opposite way from entrepreneurs. Add to this natural conservatism, a very real fear about innovation and what implications it may have for them and their position, and we have a group which may well have a major inbuilt resistance to acting in a more enterprising manner. However, in every company the collective actions of the management are critical in shaping the behaviour and attitudes of the organisation as a whole. To create the entrepreneurial company the entrepreneur needs support and input from an enterprising management team who are able, in turn, to stimulate such behaviour at all levels within the company.

The Enterprising Manager

Enterprising managers are those who are comfortable in a situation where there is ongoing change and who initiate actions or ventures which involve them in identifying the opportunities and taking action. Stump talks about managers acting as "entrepreneurial forces" in that they have a clear recognition of the future direction of the company and are able and willing to champion new ideas to move the company towards its goals. If enterprising behaviour is to take root within the company then it is crucial that managers act in this way and demonstrate to other levels that this type of behaviour is welcomed and expected.

While acknowledging the importance of the entrepreneur's style and approach in providing a lead, any significant move towards developing entrepreneurial thinking processes will be dependent upon changes in individual behaviour and attitudes. In order to start this change process we need to ensure that the following conditions are in place:

- The requirement for enterprising behaviour is known and understood.
- Managers understand what enterprising behaviour involves.
- Managers accept the need to modify their behaviour to become more enterprising.

The key to achieving the first condition lies in effective communication. Effective communication is about making things happen and this will only start to take place where the entrepreneur ensures that the management understand why the business needs to be more enterprising and the management's role in this.

The management will have to understand:

- Changes which are taking place in the market and how they may affect the company.
- The overall vision and objectives of the business.
- The changing role of the manager.
- Benchmarks against which the company should be measured.

The management must recognise the reality of the competitive context of the business and start to understand the implications it will have for their behaviour. In this initial phase the managers must know and understand the entrepreneur's perceptions of the need for change as well as moving towards accepting these needs. This is where the concept of clarity of purpose and vision for the future becomes important. There must be a clear acceptance that enterprising behaviour is critical in moving the company forward and that only through more enterprising behaviour will the company be able to achieve its goals. A shared sense of purpose between the entrepreneur and the management will reinforce this. During this phase any potential areas of resistance should be recognised and addressed before we can genuinely say that the requirement for enterprising behaviour is known and understood.

Achieving the second condition requires a recognition and understanding of the behaviours and skills which we are trying to develop. We need to understand the key competencies which make up enterprising behaviour:

- Initiative
- Commercial judgement
- Flexibility
- Creativity
- Risk-taking ability
- Autonomy
- Problem-solving ability
- Need for achievement
- Hard work
- Innovative
- Coping with ambiguity.

These attributes can be further broken down into a series of indicators which show the actions and behaviours which lie behind them (see opposite). Much traditional management training focuses on improving the skills of analysis and objectivity but neglects the development of

Competence	Indicators
Initiative	• Recognises opportunities for improvement • Seeks additional responsibility • Thrives on independence • A good leader • Requires minimal guidance
Judgement	• Good at making trade-offs between priorities • Commercial awareness • Weighs up consequences of decisions before making them • Able to distinguish between important and unimportant tasks • Seeks relevant information before making decisions
Flexibility	• Comfortable with a loosely defined job description • Balanced relationship with subordinates, other departments and customers • Copes with conflicting demands on resources • Balances freedom and control with subordinates • A good team person
Action orientation	• Can be impatient with others who do not move at same speed • Good at progressing projects • Doesn't procrastinate
Achievement	• Sets demanding goals for self and others • Shows job satisfaction • Is a self-starter • Can be consumed with a job or task • Actively influences events to achieve objectives
Innovation	• Searches for better ways to do things • Generates new ideas • Lateral thinker • Is prepared to take risks • Is continually learning
Copes with ambiguity	• Comfortable in a changing situation • Thrives under pressure • Willingly involved in the change process • An advocate of change • Good problem-solver
Competitive understanding	• Understands customer needs • Is customer-focused • Wide knowledge of the business • Relates own activities to the total business context • Aware of future external opportunities or threats

Indicators of Enterprising Competencies
(Source: Matrix; Breakthrough Management)

91

many of the attributes of enterprising behaviour, particularly in the areas of initiative, creativity and flexibility. Les O'Reilly, chairman of the Database Group, writing in the *Independent On Sunday*, commented that:

> "My biggest mistake was allowing my thorough management training to suppress my more inspirational tendencies in business.... I was a very intuitive person but was taught to look at things in an objective way. I gained an enormous amount from this training but where perhaps I went wrong was on emphasising the objective side and not giving so much attention to the 'gut feel' side."

This highlights the potential shortfalls in traditional management training when we are trying to develop more enterprising managers. The development of enterprising behaviour will require new approaches to training and development.

By understanding the needs for enterprising behaviour and the attributes which make up such behaviour, managers are starting to move towards the third condition where they accept the need to modify their behaviour towards being more enterprising.

As in any development situation there is a need to carry out an analysis of the existing skills levels within individuals or groups. We have listed the attributes of enterprising behaviour and must evaluate managers' capabilities against them. Such an analysis will allow an evaluation of the existing level of enterprising behaviour and allow training and development to be focused on the areas where there are major weaknesses. This will enhance the relevance of training and ensure that the investment in training is maximised.

The analysis of the manager's enterprising attributes should also concentrate on getting the managers to accept the key individual development areas. This is crucial because unless the individual has an intrinsic motivation to change it will be impossible to stimulate a change in attitude and behaviour.

Training and development have a major role to play in the development of enterprising managers. As we have already suggested, it is our experience that the creation of more enterprising behaviour will require major changes in attitudes as well as the development of skills and knowledge. Development of this kind requires a mix of off-the-job training, on-the-job coaching and self-development. Many of these skills and behaviours can be developed only through experience and therefore this will require a focus on action-orientated approaches to development.

Five Actions for Creating Enterprising Managers

Once the necessary conditions for change have been established there is a need to provide assistance to managers in helping them to behave in a more enterprising manner. In our experience there are a number of actions that must be taken to develop enterprising managers:

* Actions to get managers to think in an enterprising way
* Actions to create opportunities for enterprising behaviour
* Actions for the entrepreneur as role model
* Actions to reward enterprise
* Actions to recruit enterprising people.

Getting Managers to Think in an Enterprising Way

We have earlier described the importance and the characteristics of the entrepreneurial thinking process. We have to recognise that most managers do not think this way. In order to get managers to act in a more enterprising manner we need to modify thinking and move them towards a more entrepreneurial outlook. Managers have to be encouraged and developed to be aware of internal and external opportunities for developing the business. Managers have to be able to take a wider perspective than simply their own functional area or department. They need to be able to take decisions in their area, based on the widest possible business context.

There are a number of things which can be done to achieve a shift in thinking.

Keep managers close to the action. As the company grows there is a danger of the senior management becoming increasingly involved in their own functional areas and becoming distanced from the overall business situation and changes within the overall business environment. Peter Palmer, a two times successful entrepreneur, first with Spider Systems in Scotland and then the US-based Axon Network, describes this as "keeping senior managers close to the business" – not allowing them to become embroiled in bureaucracy. There is a need to keep the senior management sharp by constantly involving them in business development and market contacts.

Enhance strategic thinking. Managers must be encouraged to take a wider view of the company and its situation. They must have the ability to put the long term into perspective and recognise the strategic implications of any actions. This will require them to understand a number of strategic concepts, including:

- Vision and purpose
- The competitive situation facing the business
- Strategic focus of the business
- Basis of competitive advantage.

An awareness of these issues will not only help managers to better understand the strategic issues facing the business and how these issues relate to them and their departments, but also expose them to new concepts and models which will force them to think in a different way. The most obvious way to introduce such concepts is to involve them in the strategic decision-making process within the company. This is a useful starting point in exposing managers to strategic concepts which are directly relevant to their situation. Strategic thinking is a daily discipline and this means that managers must be exposed to situations which give them an opportunity to develop thinking processes and skills which can be employed on an ongoing basis. In the next section we shall discuss how this can be achieved.

Put the manager into a different role. A temporary transfer of a manager into a different functional area for a specific period is another way of ensuring a different perspective and encouraging a different way of thinking. The lack of resources in the smaller company may present practical difficulties in achieving this but the potential benefits in seeing the problems and issues facing others can be invaluable in forcing managers to reflect more objectively on their own department and identify potential improvements. One company needed to develop a new costing system and instead of asking the company accountant to do this, the managing director gave the task to the production director as he would be responsible for using the system. The production director had to attend a number of courses and seminars to develop his expertise in this area before he could develop the system. The end result was a costing system which was understood by production and a production director who had been forced to develop his skills and thinking in a new area.

Develop lateral thinking. The pragmatic nature of many management roles means that managers are given little opportunity or encouragement to think laterally about the issues which they are facing. Enterprising managers need to be able to think laterally and therefore thinking skills must be developed. Managers need to be given the opportunity to practise and hone such skills so that they become second nature and are utilised on a daily basis.

Bill Gates of Microsoft was asked to explain how he was able to maintain a high level of creativity from established managers. In reply he cited a number of actions which were designed to stimulate creativity:

- Regular away-days
- Encouraging brainstorming 24 hours a day through electronic mail

- Promoting informal liaison between departments
- Encouraging fun and freedom.

Focus management thinking on opportunity. According to Drucker this is a key step in introducing entrepreneurial practices. He says that "people see what is presented to them; what is not presented tends to get overlooked". Most management meetings and discussions tend to concentrate on existing and historical problems and very little time is spent on future opportunities. If we want managers to become opportunity focused then there is a need to give them an opportunity on a regular basis to think about the future. This will require separate meetings where the purpose is to think about the longer term, the potential opportunities facing the company and how they should be tackled.

Creating Opportunities for Enterprising Behaviour

Most entrepreneurs have developed their abilities and had their thinking shaped through action and experience. It would seem logical to assume that managers will only be able to become more enterprising if they are given the opportunity to act in an enterprising manner. In order to start the process of developing entrepreneurial behaviour there is a need to create situations which give the manager the opportunity to develop skills and build confidence. The leader has a major role in stimulating opportunities that challenge the manager to act in a more enterprising manner.

Exposing managers to a live business situation which forces them to act in an enterprising manner is probably the most effective way of developing the skills and confidence necessary to be enterprising. If such an experience is then analysed and reviewed with regard to the manager's performance, we have a powerful learning experience which will make the manager more effective in the future. In effect, what we are describing is a form of task-based action learning as a practical tool for getting managers to learn and develop. Mumford and others have highlighted the effectiveness of this form of on-the-job development.

The nature of the tasks will vary depending upon the role of the manager, his experience, and the skills which you wish to develop. They can range from developing a new product or market area to leading an improvement group which is aiming to improve a specific aspect of the business. The Centre for Creative Leadership has identified a range of developmental projects which are related to developing skills within existing jobs. Specific ones which relate to enterprising competencies include the following:

Helping to cope with ambiguity
• Set up a task force on a pressing business issue.
• Start up something, e.g. customer care programme, ISO 9000.
• Deal with a business crisis.
• Summarise a new trend.

Improving strategic ability
• Do a competitive analysis.
• Study innovation of customers/competitors.
• Conduct and analyse a customer questionnaire.
• Report on how present practices might be affected by future developments and trends.

Increasing independence
• Handle a negotiation with a key customer.
• Assign a project with a tight deadline.
• Go off-site to troubleshoot a problem.

These are examples of specific opportunities which can be given to managers to develop enterprising behaviour within the context of the existing role. Another way of looking at this is to examine the opportunities for enterprising behaviour as part of a continuum:

Internal task-based	Development project		Organising a separate business unit		External venture-based
		Product or market development		Spin out	

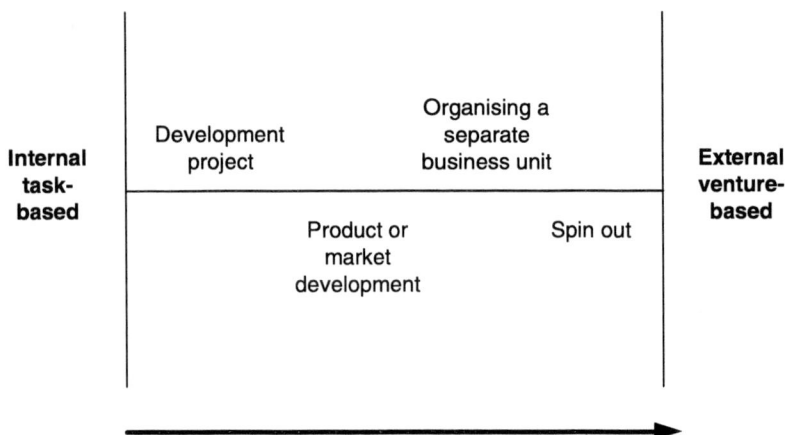

Task-based. On the left-hand side of the continuum we have a range of tasks as described in the previous section, e.g. setting up a task force on a pressing business issue or carrying out a customer-based project. These tasks can be designed to develop a particular set of attributes for the manager. As we move to the right on the continuum these tasks become much more important strategically and can include product development or the development of a new market area.

Venture-based. As we move further towards the right-hand side of the continuum we have opportunities which offer greater scope for developing more entrepreneurially-based skills. The running of a separate business unit, the commercial development of an idea to the market, and even the spin-out of a new venture to form a separate company, are all opportunities which will stretch and test the expertise of managers.

All of the opportunities on the continuum offer the scope to challenge individual managers, to stretch their capabilities and develop their enterprising skills. The opportunities which are developed will depend to some extent on the existing skills and capabilities of the management.

They should also be determined by the needs and requirements of the business.

Many companies will be content to develop managers at the left-hand side of the continuum and will see the development of more enterprising attitudes and attributes as a major step forward. As we move towards the right-hand side of the continuum we develop from enterprising towards entrepreneurial. The genuine entrepreneurial company, with its drive for flexibility and capitalising on market opportunities, requires a core of management who have the skills and confidence to commercially develop opportunities for the company.

Challenging managers through the development of venture-based opportunities offers significant benefits for the entrepreneurial company:

- It **allows market-based opportunities to be developed within the business.** In our experience the growing company is a source of many latent, market-based opportunities which are not fully exploited for a number of reasons – lack of management resources, focus on the core business, etc. Giving managers the opportunity to develop them will provide a way of testing and pushing these ideas as well as encouraging the development of enterprising behaviour.

- It **provides a way of retaining the best people.** The best managers need to be continually challenged and there is a danger in any growing company that the best people leave to pursue other opportunities, in many cases with competitors or as competitors! Allowing managers to run with interesting venture-based projects will provide a major challenge for the managers within the company.

- It **encourages market-based innovation within the company.** We have already discussed the importance of developing the capability for market-based innovation. If managers know that they will be encouraged and assisted to develop ideas and opportunities then they are more likely to be motivated towards searching and developing new ideas.

Companies such as Spectrum Associates and Virgin recognise the benefits of having managers who can operate in this way. It is the role of the leader to develop, motivate and create opportunities for management to move towards the venture side of our continuum.

Internal Competition at Spectrum

Spectrum Associates, a 150-person software company, encourages managers to "grow their own business" within Spectrum. This involves business units which develop and market their own products. The groups are allowed the freedom to pursue market opportunities as they please, but the senior management retain the decision power over the allocation of funds. Indeed, some of the products being developed within these groups are in competition with one another! John Nugent, a co-founder of the company, explains that this approach allows them to be flexible in a market where innovation is the norm. By successful he means a company that has grown by 6000 per cent in sales over the past five years.

The Entrepreneur as a Role Model

In the development of enterprising managers there is one area which is often neglected: the coaching of the manager by the entrepreneur. "Boss-derived development", as Mumford calls it, offers an opportunity for the manager to gain first-hand experience of how the entrepreneur thinks and acts.

The entrepreneur can be a positive role model and the thinking which he brings to any situation can be used to develop the individual managers' skills and thought processes. By involving managers in deals and projects in which the entrepreneur is involved, and by discussing how and why the manager makes decisions in his own area, the entrepreneur can widen the thinking of managers and increase their perspective. Many entrepreneurs complain that their managers do not think in the same way as them and this is not surprising given the different range of experiences which they undoubtedly have. How many entrepreneurs, however, have made real efforts to share their thinking and reasoning on an issue with their managers in a coaching type situation? Very few, we suspect.

One reason for this is that many entrepreneurs are uncomfortable in a coaching situation. The passive management skills involved in effective coaching – facilitating, patience, listening – are not skills which are naturally inherent in entrepreneurs. To be an effective role model the entrepreneur has to utilise a more dynamic, action-based approach which involves managers in key areas of business development and demonstrates the thought processes the entrepreneur is going through. If the entrepreneur is prepared to devote time to the development of managers then it will pay dividends in shaping their thinking. Such an approach is also likely to have an impact on motivation as enterprising managers will react positively to a closer relationship with the entrepreneur, in recognition of the skills and insights which can be picked up.

Reward Enterprising Behaviour

In our discussions with entrepreneurs on what motivates them, although monetary reward is not the prime motivator in most cases, financial independence and the opportunity to generate above average rewards are major drivers. This is the same with employees. Although there are a number of reasons why people want to be more enterprising – more satisfying work, sense of achievement, recognition and status with boss and peers – the financial rewards should not be forgotten.

The nature of the reward has to be linked to the nature of the enterprising behaviour and the impact which it has on the performance of the company. In the situation where enterprising behaviour leads to specific internal improvements there is a need to consider one-off or ongoing individual or team bonuses. If we have enterprising behaviour which creates new streams of revenue for the company, either in terms of new market opportunities or new products or services, then we need to consider different ways of rewarding people. More and more companies are becoming involved in profit-sharing schemes and increasingly entrepreneurs are recognising the need to involve key people by selling them a stake in the business.

Genuine entrepreneurial companies recognise the importance of rewards. It has been suggested that the Virgin Group has created at least a dozen millionaires among its executives. Spectrum Associates give their employees a significant share of the revenues which their products generate. Such approaches reinforce the value of enterprising behaviour within the company and lock key executives into the company.

The old truism of "you get more of what you reward" is just as applicable in the situation of the entrepreneurial company and therefore we have to be clear about what rewards we give and the signals which are being sent out by them. Reward systems need to be thought through and their implications need to be carefully considered. In the successful entrepreneurial company there are systems which reward performance which moves the company towards its goals.

Recruit Enterprising Managers

Much of what we have written about in regard to creating enterprising managers is to do with developing attitudes and behaviours. This process can be made much easier if we are starting with individuals who show some inclination towards enterprise. Although we can improve most people's performance through development and the creation of an environment which stimulates enterprise, we have to recognise that some managers will have limitations in taking on board some aspects of enterprising behaviour. This is particularly true if we are starting at the opposite end of the enterprise continuum, with managers who display the thinking processes of classic managers.

Wouldn't the whole process be much easier if we had recruited enterprising managers in the first place? The answer is of course yes, and we could make this process much easier by recruiting managers who display, or show potential, for enterprising behaviour. Growth brings opportunities to augment the existing management team with new managers who can bring different skills and perspectives to the entrepreneurial company. One entrepreneur suggests that she concentrates on recruiting high-energy, highly intelligent people who are prepared for constant change and are comfortable in situations which are not traditional. Our experience in growing companies and interviews with successful entrepreneurs has shown us the importance of the recruitment of capable managers who are able to buy into the entrepreneur's vision for the company and be enterprising in their approach to helping the company to achieve it.

The need to recruit enterprising managers calls for a review of the existing recruitment procedures and criteria, and being prepared to recruit people who are demanding and will challenge the existing norms within the company. As well as functional ability, we need to be testing for enterprising characteristics and searching for evidence of a track record of innovation and enterprising behaviour in previous employment. Good recruitment will not eliminate the need for development of enterprising behaviour but it is likely to accelerate the process and give better results more quickly. While recognising the issue of loyalty to long-serving employees and individuals who are functionally skilled but enterprise-averse, we have to understand that unless managers are committed to becoming more enterprising, the longer-term effectiveness of the business will be constrained.

In order to allow enterprising behaviour within the company the leaders must be prepared to display patience. Developing new attitudes can be a major cultural change and will take time. Creating enterprising people will have a long-term benefit for the company and therefore should not be seen as a "quick fix", but rather an ongoing process over a significant period which will require patience and support from the top.

The Technology Partnership:
Success Through People

The Technology Partnership was formed in 1988 by Gerald Avison and 24 others who created a business which provided strategic consultancy. The business used the cash flow and expertise provided by the consultancy to allow it to develop its own products. Gradually the consultancy is becoming a manufacturer.

Today the business has over 160 employees and was deemed by 3i as the company with the greatest growth potential in the 90s. It has developed a number of world-leading technologies which allow it to compete with some of the major companies in its chosen areas. The Technology Partnership is one of a new breed of entrepreneurial companies which has developed market opportunities through flexibility and the enterprising nature of its people.

Within the company responsibility is devolved to the lowest level which is able to accept it. Avison believes that the freedom, motivation and responsibility levels of the employees make it very difficult for large companies to compete against it.

The company tries to recruit the best people and it rewards them with a share of the business. More than 70 per cent of the business is owned by the directors and the staff.

Chapter 6

Organising for Enterprise

While the development of enterprising managers and enterprising people at all levels of the organisation requires the development of attitudes, skills and knowledge, we also have to work hard at creating an organisational environment which supports and stimulates enterprising behaviour.

Sadler has described the basic elements of any organisation as structure, systems and procedures and values and culture. He describes structure as covering the formal channels for reporting and allocating responsibility; systems and procedures as the methods for information processing, decision-making and taking action; and values and culture relate to how things are done and what behaviours are encouraged. Our earlier description of the entrepreneurial company covered two areas which are related to these organisation issues:

- There is a management culture in which entrepreneurial behaviour is so deeply valued that it drives people's thinking and actions.

- There are flexible, customer-focused structures which enhance and sustain entrepreneurial behaviour.

In discussing how we organise for enterprise we need to consider both of these areas.

The culture of any company is the set of shared values beliefs and norms which give the business its character and differentiate it from other businesses. In the entrepreneurial company the main influence on the culture is the values and vision of the entrepreneur. Much of our previous chapters on Leadership and Creating Enterprising People is about developing the culture of the business.

A key topic which links culture and structure is empowerment. Empowerment is about developing a culture that encourages people to take responsibility for their actions and providing an organisation structure which allows this.

The Importance of Empowerment

Any organisation which wishes to become flexible, responsive and continually improving must develop people who are flexible, responsive and open to improvement. This will only happen where individuals take ownership for decisions and responsibility for actions. Empowering people is a key aspect of developing such individuals.

The empowerment of employees has to be the way forward for entrepreneurial companies as without it the responsibility for decision-making and changes will always be seen as the senior management's role. If only a relatively small group within the company (the senior management) are involved in decision-making and innovation, then the capacity of the organisation to react and make improvements will be much less than a similar-sized organisation where all of the people are fully empowered.

At its simplest empowerment is about giving power to those who have never had it, charging individuals with the ability to make decisions about key aspects of their work without seeking the "permission" of those above them. On a more complex level empowerment is at the heart of a more subtle approach to leadership which is based upon changing needs of organisations and a changing shift in the aspirations employees have from their work.

In successful entrepreneurial companies an integral part of any job is the ability to innovate and constantly improve how things are done. Changing attitudes towards this way of thinking is the responsibility of the management, who must constantly strive to push decision-making down the organisation and increase real responsibility.

There are a number of major benefits of empowerment:

- It encourages people at all levels within the company to take ownership of decisions and to contribute to improvements.
- It frees up management time and allows management to focus on more developmental issues.
- It allows faster decision-making and therefore greater company flexibility.

Key issues relating to empowerment are:

Decreasing Control and Increasing Effectiveness

Empowerment involves pushing decision-making down the organisation to give individuals responsibility in areas where previously they may only have had limited or no involvement in the decision-making process. This does not involve giving up control but rather changing the way in which it is exercised. The direct power of managers may reduce but both productivity and motivation should increase. Productivity increases come about due to reduced decision-making times and better implementation due to decisions being made by the implementor, thus ensuring greater commitment. Motivation will improve due to greater involvement and ownership of decisions about aspects of the individual's or team's work.

A Series of Learning Steps

It must be recognised that empowerment does not happen overnight. The degree to which empowerment can take place depends on the existing culture within the organisation, the management style employed and the attitudes and capabilities of the employees. Changes must be incremental, learned from, and built upon with the necessary support and training provided to the workforce. If this does not take place there is a danger of the process being stifled due to the increased expectations of management not matching the capabilities of employees.

Empowerment and Learning Are Inextricably Linked

Real empowerment will only take place in a situation where people want to improve themselves and the organisation. There is a direct link between people wanting to improve themselves and working to improve how they do their job. As responsibility is pushed down to individuals they must be expanding their capabilities to handle the responsibility and make best use of it. This will only happen in a situation where people want to learn.

People within an organisation must be given an opportunity to improve by the availability of learning opportunities. Management must strive to create a learning organisation. According to Mumford such an organisation can be described as follows:

- Encourages managers to identify their own learning needs
- Provides a regular feedback and review of performance and learning
- Encourages individuals to set challenging goals
- Seeks to provide new learning experiences
- Provides or facilitates the use of training on the job
- Encourages the review and planning of learning activities

A leadership and management focus on stimulating and supporting empowerment will be a practical starting point in developing a management culture in which entrepreneurial behaviour is so deeply valued that it drives people's thinking and actions.

Flexibility and Structure

Most management thinking supports the premise that structure should follow strategy. In the next section on entrepreneurial strategies we shall discuss the opportunistic nature of strategy development in the entrepreneurial company. We also suggest that strategy should be underpinned by a closeness to customers and markets. To achieve both of these conditions the structure of the entrepreneurial company needs to offer an inherent flexibility to respond to changes in customer requirements and their subsequent impact on strategies. Also, structure has to be able to facilitate and provide support for risk-taking, proactive behaviour and innovation throughout the company.

Flexibility in structure is a relatively new concept and calls for a move away from the mechanistic, hierarchical model which has been the basis for most organisational design in the past. Different forms of organisational structure have been evolving to create flexibility within organisations.

The Inverted Triangle

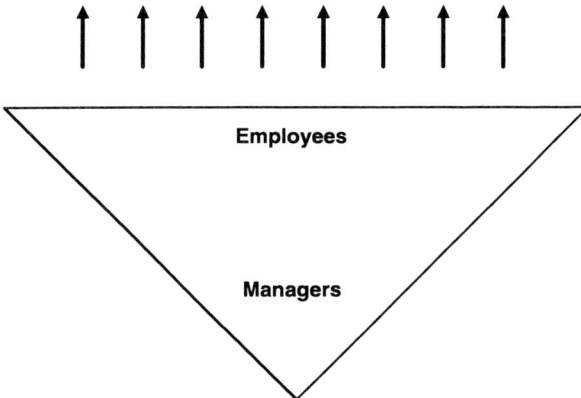

↑ ↑ ↑ ↑ ↑ ↑ ↑ ↑

Employees

Managers

In the traditional hierarchical structure the manager is seen at the apex of the triangle, leading and controlling a group of subordinates. The inverted triangle is based upon the belief that the key to achieving company objectives on an ongoing basis is the manager's ability to empower subordinates and to see subordinates as the key to interfacing with customers. By inverting the triangle the manager's role is to support employees, ensuring that they have the necessary resources to achieve their objectives. This model suggests that management does not fit at the top of the hierarchy, but that management primacy must come second to group needs.

Cloverleaf Organisations

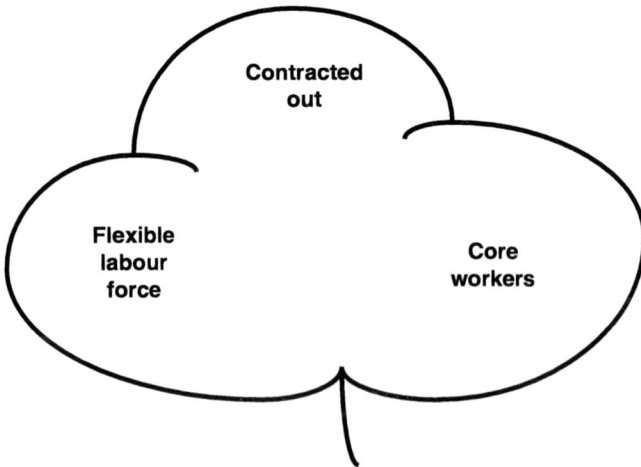

Charles Handy suggests that organisations will take on a cloverleaf shape, the centre of which will be a small professional core team and the outer leaves made up of a flexible labour force of part-time and contract workers as well as contracting out and subcontracting a major proportion of work. Such an organisation structure is seen as reducing the overheads of the organisation and increasing its ability to react to environmental change.

Responses to Complexity

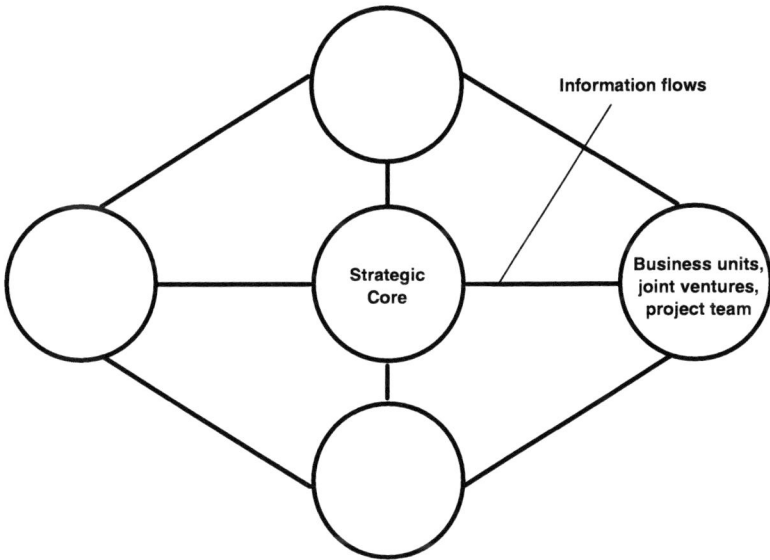

Daniel Power has identified a number of new organisational structures which have been developed in response to increasingly complex environments. He describes models without conventional hierarchies which can be developed due to advances in information technology; organisations which are split into a number of autonomous operating units linked by sophisticated information and communication networks; and organisations which are made up of a complex network of interrelated business units, project teams and joint ventures.

Each of these organisational types and structures has been developed as a response to ongoing change and a recognition that traditional models have severe limitations when they are faced with a need for increasing flexibility and fast response. If the entrepreneurial company is to evolve a structure which allows it to grow while retaining flexibility then consideration must be given to different forms of structure such as those described above.

Slevin and Covin have found that there is a key relationship between entrepreneurial behaviour and the type of structure within a company. They have shown that entrepreneurial behaviour correlates positively with the presence of an organic organisational structure while a mechanistic organisation structure has a negative impact on entrepreneurial behaviour.

An organic organisation structure can be described as follows:

• Open communication channels with a free flow of information
• A variety and flexibility in operating styles
• Decision authority based on the expertise of the individual
• Free adaptation by the organisation to changing circumstances
• Focus is on getting things done and is unconstrained by procedures
• Loose, informal control
• Flexible on-job behaviour
• Consultation and participation encouraged.

Growing companies can probably relate to many of these characteristics as their size and lack of complexity lend themselves towards an organic rather than mechanistic structure. However, some of the characteristics and ways of doing things which we take for granted when the company is small, need to be worked at as the business develops. Also, the drive towards introducing systems and procedures to control and manage growth may be moving the company towards a more a more mechanistic structure. If this happens, the emphasis on the way of doing business will shift towards a uniformity, rigidity and structured approach which may diminish the company's ability to be entrepreneurial.

In developing a structure there are a number of issues which must be considered.

Structures Which Are Customer-Focused

Although there is a close link between strategy and structure, the major driving force for strategy in the entrepreneurial company is customer and market requirements. This means that the major influence on organisational structure is customers. In our experience the structure of many companies is based on internal considerations with a focus on building on what is there and developing a structure which suits the existing operations. Entrepreneurial companies need to take an external perspective, organising themselves by identifying what the most appropriate structure is to meet existing customer needs and to be able to respond to changing requirements.

In some situations the links with the customers are so close that the structures of both organisations can be interlinked. Employees are becoming part of customer's operations and project teams, and information technology links between customers and suppliers are becoming commonplace. These linkages force companies to consider how their structure meshes with that of their customers.

Structures Built on Networks Not Hierarchies

Every company, large and small, depends on informal networks to get things done to a greater or larger extent. These networks are based on relationships between individuals and groups within departments and across functional areas. Such networks are used to get round the inertia of formal systems and procedures which can slow down responses or decisions. Often these relationships are at best tolerated and the formal systems are seen as the main route for decision-making. Companies which create flexibility in their structures recognise the importance of networks and find ways of legitimising them by encouraging their development and removing any barriers or constraints. In such a situation there is likely to be:

* A lack of formal organisation charts and job descriptions
* Authority is based on influence not job title
* Overlap between jobs and departments
* Fuzzy boundaries between departments
* Flat structure with dual reporting relationships
* New pieces of the organisation are created around key people.

113

This creates a dynamic organisation which is well set to respond quickly to change. However, this type of structure can also be difficult to manage as it calls for individuals who are comfortable and confident in dealing with ambiguity. There is also a danger of some confusion and uncertainty as traditional roles and power bases are challenged.

Structures Which Encourage Teamwork and Collaboration

Flexibility and responsiveness to the needs of customers requires an organisation where everyone is working towards a common goal. Decisions and accountability can be enhanced if there is a focus on teams rather than individuals and the accent is on genuine collaboration. Collaboration involves the understanding that in any successful company 'no man is an island'. Companies are not made up of collections of individuals working on their own but rather by a complex series of interconnected processes and interrelations where people depend on each other. People must recognise that their ability to perform their jobs successfully is dependent upon other individuals and groups.

Teamwork and collaboration also ensures the benefits from the increased range of skills, experience and perspectives that a number of individuals, working together, can bring to achieving an objective or accomplishing a task.

Collaboration involves:

- Sharing responsibility for actions and outcomes
- Group problem-solving
- Recognition of other people's problems and issues.

Structures which encourage teamwork and collaboration are typified by:

- Collaborative objective setting
- Systems which encourage wide access to, and sharing of, information
- Group reward systems
- Cross-functional improvement groups.

114

Creative Use of Information Technology

The increasing power and decreasing cost of IT means that it has a major role to play in assisting the creation of more flexible structures. Sophisticated management information systems allow access to a wide range of information which can be used to facilitate and speed up decision processes while interactive communication systems allow rapid dissemination and exchange of information.

IT has an 'enabling' role in allowing structural flexibility by allowing individuals and teams to operate with more autonomy and speed. Greater use of IT also allows management to monitor the performance of these autonomous groups and to build in 'early warning' systems and measures to identify potential problems.

Structure and Size

More and more companies are recognising that there is a fundamental link between flexibility and size. The larger the organisation becomes the more difficult it is to build in inherent flexibility. As companies grow there is a tendency to become more bureaucratic.

The sheer logistics of size means that as companies employ more people and increase formal systems and procedures, then it will be more difficult to retain flexibility. As a company becomes bigger it is more difficult to retain the sense of purpose throughout the business and individuals can lose the feeling that their personal contribution matters.

However, in most business sectors there are economies which can be derived through a certain scale of operations. Management has to understand their industry and identify what is the optimal size which will create economies of scale but still allow flexibility. Increasingly this is being achieved by splitting companies up into smaller units or developing separate companies when the core business reaches a certain size. The creative use of joint ventures is also a way of smaller companies benefiting from economies of scale in distribution while retaining a size which benefits from flexibility.

Structuring For Growth

The Leith agency is one of the leading growing advertising agencies in the UK. The business was established nine years ago and in 1993 the founding Managing Director, John Denholm, started to look at where the business was heading. He recognised that the advertising business was changing with increasing demands from customers for a wider range of services.

While these services could have been developed within the scope of the original business (as other agencies have tried to do), Denholm was also concerned with size. The business was growing fast and he was concerned that if it got too big it would be difficult to retain the culture and creativity which made the business successful in the first place.

The solution was to set up a new holding company and 'spin out' a number of companies from within the advertising agency. Key individuals were recruited or moved from the agency to head up these separate companies. There are now four companies in the group, including the original agency, a direct marketing company, a graphics company and design specialists. There is also a central finance and personnel service which provides these services to all of the group companies.

There have been major benefits of this approach with profits and turnover increasing, an ability to provide a wider range of services to clients while retaining the character, creativity and flexibility of the individual companies.

Those organisations with flexible structures will be best placed to sustain continuous development. Entrepreneurial companies must be prepared continually to review and redesign their organisational structure in response to the changes in strategies brought about by changing customer and market requirements.

The drives towards these new paradigms of company management are nowhere more apparent than in the larger organisation. Under attack from new entrants and fleet-of-foot technology-based competitors, the big corporations are delayering, downsizing and re-engineering. In essence many are seeking to emulate the responsiveness of the small company. Asea Brown Boveri (AB&B), the giant industrial firm whose £30 billion annual turnover is now managed through 3,000 operating companies, is one of the most radical restructurings of this kind. From such examples it can be seen that the most sought-after ideal company would be a dynamic mid-sized company.

Tom Peters, in many of his writings and speeches, refers to this current economic time as the era of the "gazelle". The connotations are of speed, responsiveness, alertness and a supernatural ability to leap across new terrain. Less poetically there is a clear desire for large companies to attain something of the dynamic of the small company. At the heart of this quest lie people and behaviour.

Around the mid-eighties Peter Drucker, the corporatist guru, was not only acknowledging this shift but was proclaiming the need for it:

"Today's businesses, especially the large ones, simply will not survive in this period of rapid change and innovation unless they acquire entrepreneurial competence". (From *Innovation and Entrepreneurship*, 1985)

Large corporations may be able to reinvent themselves into a string of little companies as the case of AB & B has shown. This structural shift will have profound impacts on the way in which their business gets done. A structural answer is not of itself the total solution. Larger companies and corporations are looking to find ways to utilise the (latent) capabilities of their workforce as they cope with the demands of increasing competition. These demands in turn have created a new "agenda" for success. The winners will be those who can best handle innovation – and by innovation we mean doing new things rather than "invention". This in turn leads into the ability which companies must have to "manage the new". Managing the new is far from managing the current. The new has uncertainty, doubt and risk at its core.

Intrapreneurship

It is a very short step from this insight to see that large companies and corporations have to become more "entrepreneurial" in order to manage the new agenda. To give shape to this notion a new word has emerged – an intrapreneur. The intrapreneur is someone who acts in an entrepreneurial way but doesn't leave the company.

The Nature of Intrapreneurship

Corporate entrepreneurship, or intrapreneurship, is a concept that has acquired more and more importance in recent years. Serious academic work has been documented to describe the phenomenon, and more and more business gurus have commented on the value of the corporate entrepreneur.

In some ways this surge of interest has coincided with the increasing legitimacy of the study of entrepreneurship itself. It has been clear to many that the main traits associated with entrepreneurial activity – i.e. growth, innovation and flexibility – are equally attractive to large organisations, and hence the notion of developing entrepreneurship in corporations became a focus for academic and commercial efforts.

Although many writers have now explored the topic of intrapreneurship, the seminal work is attributed to Gifford Pinchot III. In this book *Intrapreneuring*, he describes the activities of people in a range of organisations, though predominantly Hewlett-Packard and 3M Corporation in the USA, ranging back to the mid-1960s. In these case histories, Pinchot details the ways in which individuals achieved significant innovative breakthroughs in developing new products and processes, most often *despite* the planning, coordination, and control mechanisms of the organisation within which they worked. In some cases these new products or services were then taken through to full commercial realisation by a spin-off company, usually involving the original intrapreneur.

In this way, intrapreneurship has been associated mostly with the notion of the "corporate entrepreneur" who, quite literally in some cases, defies the recognised practices and procedures of the host organisation, taking significant risks in the process, to incubate a pet idea for a new product, service or process. In so doing the intrapreneur is likely to utilise corporate resources to develop technology or market intelligence, as well as significant periods of his or her own time.

In his book Pinchot describes how Hewlett-Packard and 3M have both attempted to "institutionalise" the practice of intrapreneurship by adopting organisational and management practices specifically aimed at encouraging and supporting the intrapreneur, and how these practices have very much served to form the distinctive cultures that these organisations are now associated with.

From our own work in this field we see that the scope for intrapreneurship is large. Many companies could use so much more of their people's latent innovation and entrepreneurial ability. Yet the application of such an approach can be a major shift for many companies. People acting intrapreneurially will by necessity create upset, by bringing change and not doing things in the conventional way. To have an entrepreneurial culture in a large organisation you need something like the following:

- The opportunity for "entrepreneurs" to come from any functional area and any level within the company.
- Coaching and mentoring to bring ideas into revenue streams.
- True and full empowerment. This means the possibility that the intrapreneurs can participate in the profit return of the successful projects.
- A defeated corporate immune system. Support from the top is essential to overcome the potential for good ideas to be stifled and the corporate immune system to reject anything new or foreign.

These are quite some challenges! But, the rewards can be awesome. Using the Foresight Group methodology, of which we are part, companies are able to get to their first customer with greater speed, lower costs and greater zeal than conventional corporate processes for NPD or innovation.

A case study will help to illustrate this. The Bell Atlantic Phone Company adopted this methodology and achieved the following results:

- 150 latent intrapreneurs lured out of hiding
- New business ideas "moonlighted"
- Generated 90 projects
- 30 active projects forecast $100,000,000 revenue over five years
- 15 new products in the marketplace after three years.

This was achieved by a mixture of "training" to help the would-be intrapreneurs "fail their way to success", direct counselling to find creative ways to exploit opportunity and large-scale commitment from the top to support the fledgling ideas. The wider benefits of such an approach are that the company culture is now much more pro experimentation and "risk". Specifically the approach deals with:

- Idea and business opportunity development
- Entrepreneurial skill development – creative frugality
- Researching the unknown
- Stakeholders and corporate politics
- Support for pre-commercialisation.

For the intrapreneurs who participate it becomes a tangible reality that there is scope to utilise all their creative talents in their corporation. Corporations who take up the "Champion Programme", as the methodology is called, are required to make the big shift both to allow people from any point in the company become a champion and to reward them accordingly.

Part 4

Entrepreneurship and Market-Based Strategy

Chapter 7

Entrepreneurial Strategy

We earlier described the ability and drive to create businesses as being the prime motivators for the serial entrepreneur. We also suggested that this was a major development area for emerging entrepreneurs. The development of entrepreneurial strategies – ways of achieving the entrepreneur's vision – is a critical aspect of building businesses. The action orientation of entrepreneurs means that the approaches they take to strategy development are distinctive and a key element of the entrepreneurial company.

Effective strategies and the ability to apply strategic thinking on an ongoing basis are core elements of any successful company. Strategy is about how companies achieve their objectives and how they create an advantage within the marketplace. For entrepreneurs to be effective in the area of strategic development requires an understanding of the distinct approach to strategic development which is displayed in the entrepreneurial company and an understanding of the key issues which underpin successful strategy in such companies.

The strategic development of the entrepreneurial company has been described as unstructured, irregular and informal. Certainly the strategic process is very unlike the corporate planning process with its clear systematic approach to goal setting, structured analysis, long-term planning horizon and formal measures of progress. The strategic planning approach of large companies involves a time-consuming process where the focus is on minimising risk and eliminating uncertainty before making strategic decisions.

The entrepreneurial approach involves an iterative approach to strategy which follows the credo of:

READY.......FIRE.......AIM

This approach is action-based with constant small-scale probing and experimentation to develop strategies and strategic approaches. In this way strategic approaches are continually being evolved and modified.

Strategy development in an entrepreneurial company can be described as having the following characteristics:

Intuitive rather than analytical. Strategies are based on the entrepreneur's "feel" for the market and although this may be based on an ongoing appraisal of a changing situation any analysis is more likely to be subconscious than structured.

Informality rather than formality. Many entrepreneurs have an antipathy towards formal "strategic planning" and most believe that the ability to be opportunistic is more important than planning. Hence flexibility and action will tend to supersede analysis and planning.

Short-term strategies with long-term focus. Ongoing changes in the external environment and the opportunistic nature of the entrepreneurial company mean that strategic approaches are continually adapted and modified. This means that although the overall vision may be long-term, strategic approaches may only be constant in the short term.

Ambition driven rather than condition driven. The driver for strategy is the vision and ambition of the entrepreneur. Although the strategy may change the overall goal remains constant. This means that although the strategy may be modified in the light of changes in the market or environment, the main drive will continue to be determined by the entrepreneur's vision.

From our experience of working with entrepreneurs it is clear that strategy in entrepreneurial companies is seen as a living thing, constantly subject to realignment and reappraisal in the light of changing market environments and customer needs. One entrepreneur described strategy to us as "the visible evidence of the entrepreneur's thought process, where the goal is constant but the strategy changes constantly". This clarity of focus is critical or else there is no foundation for strategic decision-making and changes in the strategic approach. Indeed, strategy should be seen as the visible evidence of the thinking processes which the successful entrepreneur is continually involved in.

This distinctive entrepreneurial approach to strategy has a number of benefits:

- Strategy is seen as an ongoing process and therefore encourages flexibility in thinking and actions
- It supports a fast response to changes in the environment
- It provides a clear strategic focus towards an overall company vision.

A key aspect of entrepreneurs' approach to building a business is opportunism. They continually scan their environment to seek out opportunities. One entrepreneur described his approach as "hungrily searching for opportunities". These opportunities can arise in a number of ways:

- Outsourcing
- Customers looking for additional suppliers
- Geographical transfer of an idea
- Tapping unused resources
- Where large companies relinquish a market
- Complacency from existing companies

- Rule or legislative changes
- New technology changing and creating markets.

A key aspect of many of these areas is change. The bigger the change the bigger the opportunity and it is no surprise that many entrepreneurs and entrepreneurial companies have emerged from markets which have undergone radical structural shifts. For example, Stagecoach, led by Ann Gloag and Brian Soutar, have capitalised on deregulation in the transport industry. Wiseman Dairies in the early 1970s were a small family business and now employ over 2000 people in a market which has undergone substantial change in distribution and buying practices.

Entrepreneurial companies thrive in situations where there is constructive or deconstructive change – market areas which could be considered as emerging or growth-oriented or traditional areas in which there has been significant upheaval due to changes in technology, legislation or other external forces. The exploitation of such opportunities is dependent upon strategic flexibility in thinking and actions.

Genuine entrepreneurs have the intuitive skills that Mintzberg describes as "seeing ahead and seeing beyond" – the abilities to not only foresee the future but also to construct the future itself, by creating products and markets to meet unforeseen (by the majority) needs. Entrepreneurs have the ability to spot and sense changing patterns within markets and trends which are developing.

Another key aspect of strategy in the entrepreneurial company is flexibility. *Inc.* magazine's study into the 500 top growing US companies stated that the most striking finding was the extent to which they had grown because of their willingness to change plans and directions. According to *Inc.*, "These entrepreneurs have flourished because of their willingness to be flexible and to follow changing markets towards growth. If one product or service proved too mature or too competitive they'd often shift resources to another, related market in an earlier stage of the product life cycle or seek some submarket in which they could compete more effectively." *Inc.* suggests the process of developing a fast-moving entrepreneurial company is one of trial and error, from a strategic perspective.

Entrepreneurial companies display an adaptive flexibility that enables them to move quickly to align themselves with opportunities. Richard Branson describes the strategy for the Virgin Group as being "freewheeling" in that one thing just leads to another: record shops to record labels to recording studios. The search for opportunities is neither random nor unstructured in that it is based on a well developed entrepreneurial antenna which is focused on paying attention to the market and noticing shifts in patterns and trends. Gerald Avison of The Technology Partnership talks about "planned opportunism" and "rattling around in the marketplace" to develop a focus and areas of expertise. These approaches combine the intuitive skills of the entrepreneur with strategic thinking and planning skills which are honed by the changing requirements of customers and markets.

In the entrepreneurial company the informal, flexible and opportunistic approaches to strategy may appear to be unstructured and seem not to fit into many established strategic models. However, it is our view that there are a number of issues which underpin strategic development in successful entrepreneurial companies:

- Innovative ways of doing business
- A focus on niche strategies
- Close to the customer
- Developing strategy capability.

Innovative Ways of Doing Business

At a recent conference on the topic of Successful Growth Companies, one speaker made a very persuasive case for successful companies being those which "satisfy unsatisfied customer needs uniquely well". Remember Gio Benedetti and "selling differences"? One of the main characteristics of successful entrepreneurial companies is their uniqueness: their capacity to find and capitalise on innovative ways of doing business. The ability to develop innovative strategies and approaches to

127

tackling markets and serving customers are key characteristics of the entrepreneurial company.

The entrepreneurial company displays a number of advantages in the area of developing innovative strategies:

- The ability to react quickly to market opportunities
- Dynamic entrepreneurial management
- Ingenuity and flexibility in thinking
- Closeness to customers.

The true entrepreneurial company is able to capitalise on these advantages in creating innovative strategies. Most people would accept the need for innovation in companies and recognise that if companies could be more innovative then they will be well placed to be more competitive. A company that is innovative will be improving on how things are done, making things better or promoting itself more successfully.

A joint survey by the CBI and the Department of Trade and Industry, *Innovation, The Best Practice*, showed that innovative firms tended to have larger market shares, higher growth rates and sustainable profits. However, to understand how innovation is applied to strategy development in the entrepreneurial company we need to define the concept more clearly.

Innovation is the purposeful application of new ideas. In the context of business strategy this means creating a market advantage through differentiation either in product uniqueness or in different ways of doing business. Innovation is not just invention! There are a numerous innovative approaches which can be developed by the entrepreneurial company and these include product invention, creating a product or service which did not exist before, modifying existing products and devising new ways of doing business. Innovation can also transform products or services which are in decline.

One of the main drivers for market-based innovation is the recognition that successful companies have to able to offer or develop something different. It is only when you clearly differentiate your business or open up a new way of doing business that you will be able to generate above average profits. The genuine entrepreneurial company doesn't operate in a "me too" environment. They are interested in areas where they can generate substantial returns and this requires innovation. Typical entrepreneurial approaches to strategy are described below.

Marketing Innovation

This involves finding new ways to present existing products or services to the market. It can involve repackaging or repositioning products, identifying new users for existing products, developing different distribution channels or different marketing approaches. Examples of these types of approaches can be found in the mail order industry where the direct selling of a range of products from flowers to nappies has opened up new opportunities for a number of fairly standard products. A specific example is Direct Line, which has had spectacular success in the direct selling of motor insurance through a mixture of marketing innovation allied to the utilisation of new technology. The success of this approach has led to the founder, Peter Wood, becoming the highest-paid executive in the UK.

Non-Standard Service

This involves differentiation through the development of service excellence. It involves understanding customer expectations and then being prepared to continually surprise and delight customers by exceeding their requirements. This is the approach undertaken by One Devonshire Gardens, the small Glasgow-based hotel which was the Egon Ronay Hotel of the Year in 1993.

Customer Partnership

As many large companies seek to rationalise their supplier base, entrepreneurial companies are picking up on this opportunity by developing approaches which involve searching for growth customers and aligning the business to them. The objective of this approach is to create a genuine partnership by fulfilling customer needs in a way which makes you indispensable. The relationship between The Lane Group haulage company and the Body Shop is an example of how a business has been developed on the back of a close-knit relationship with a growing customer.

Niche Dominance

The increasing rate of change in most markets and increasing requirements for specialisation have created increasing opportunities for niche approaches. We shall discuss the importance of niche strategies in the next section but here we highlight the importance of niche dominance as an entrepreneurial approach. La Forniaia is a specialist bakery company which supplies many of the retail multiples with innovative bread products. According to the MD, Peggy Czyzak, they have created a unique niche which is attractive to others. The way they are keeping ahead is by being very creative in terms of reaction to the market place and developing new products.

Low-Risk Entry

This approach involves finding ways of reducing the potential risks of moving into a new area by developing low-cost methods of market entry. This can involve setting up organisations which concentrate on marketing while subcontracting other elements such as production or distribution, or using distribution agreements and joint ventures to gain market knowledge and presence while sharing risk. The Technology Partnership is a good example where the cash flow and experience gained as a consultancy was used to support the development of world-class techniques and a move into manufacture.

Each of the approaches discussed above shows ways that entrepreneurs and their companies can differentiate themselves from their competitors through innovation. A key theme which arises time and time again in such companies is creativity. The ability to spot new ways of doing things and to find creative ways of adding value to your customer is a critical aspect of becoming more entrepreneurial.

Focus on Niche Strategies

Niche markets are the domain of the entrepreneurial company. Market niches offer the opportunity to provide a specialist product or service to a specific market segment.

A true market niche is not simply a market segment or a group of customers. In our view a genuine market niche is a market segment with low competitive pressure and relatively small groups of customers. This is different from an open market or even a segment of an open market that may have a small number of customers but significant competitive pressure. This narrow definition of a niche is important as only a true niche will offer the competitive benefits which a niche focus can allow. The niche strategist seeks market opportunities which, as far as possible, meets this definition.

Many market segments which were originally niches have evolved away from this as more competition moves into the market. Niche markets are dynamic market segments which are continually changing.

The main benefits of niche strategies are:

Avoiding Head-to-Head Competition with Larger Competitors

In an open market the small entrepreneurial company can often be at a major disadvantage to larger companies which have substantial resources and investment capability. In any market large companies do not tend to cover the full spectrum because it is not effective for them to do so. They tend to concentrate on the segments which are large enough to generate significant sales and returns. This leaves gaps which offer opportunities for smaller organisations to develop while minimising the potential competitive reaction, at least in the short term.

Niches Offer Decreased Competition

A genuine niche has low levels of competitive pressure with few competitors, either because the niche is of no interest to larger competitors or because no one else has identified or exploited the particular market area. The true niche player is looking to establish a high percentage of market share as quickly as possible, to allow them to dominate the niche. Developing a market dominance can establish entry barriers which discourage other companies from entering the niche. Dominance also builds up considerable market expertise and customer understanding which can be used to defend the niche against existing competitors or potential entrants.

Niches Allow a Focus on Margins, Not Volume

The major justification for niche strategies is that they allow the development of specialised or differentiated products or services which allow better margins than those which are available in an open market. The lack of competition and the product/service uniqueness mean that cost-based considerations are not of prime importance and therefore there is the opportunity for above average margins.

From these benefits we can list the characteristics of the ideal niche market. These are:

* Of minimal interest to large competitors
* Has growth potential
* Allows a focus on margin, not volume
* Is of a size which offers potential for development
* Is defendable.

The starting point in developing any niche strategy is to be able to spot the opportunity. This involves the ability to identify market segments which are being missed or to recognise where market trends and changes in customer requirements are creating new segments.

132

Whenever a niche has been identified, speed of development is critical to ensure the benefits described above. Developing the niche to a sustainable size and creating niche dominance as quickly as possible are the twin objectives in the initial implementation of a niche strategy.

Whenever a niche has been established the above average margins are bound to attract the interest of other companies. When this happens the options for the entrepreneurial company are clear: sell or defend. The entrepreneurial company which has achieved niche dominance is well placed to defend its position, even against larger entrants. This involves using the intimate knowledge it should have about the customers and the market to build customer loyalty through a focus on service excellence or to "shift the goal posts" by modifying the product or service to provide greater value. Only by continually developing the market through adding greater value to customers or shifting the basis of competition, will the entrepreneurial company keep ahead of the competition.

Even where the preferred option is to sell, the entrepreneurial company may still have to initially defend the market niche to convince any potential entrant of the difficulties of competing with an established company.

In short, we can see that the key skills necessary to be a successful niche player could be described as market awareness, opportunism and flexibility. These are exactly the characteristics which should be inherent in the entrepreneurial company.

Niche Focus on Socks!

HJ Sock Group are a fourth-generation family hosiery firm which manufactures socks. When Peter Hall took over from his father in 1989 the turnover was around £5 million with profits of around £700,000. Over a period of five or so years the turnover increased to £9 million with a profit in excess of £1 million. This was achieved against a background of extremely difficult trading for the British sock industry.

(continued overleaf)

Niche Focus on Socks! (contd)

The sock is an item which could be seen as the definitive me-too product in an open market where competition is intense. However, HJ Sock Group's success is built on a strategy of identifying and developing market niches and in finding innovation-based technological breakthroughs which differentiate them from the more generic sock markets. They have focused their efforts on small market segments for which the specialist requirements were unlikely to be met by bulk manufacturers, such as professional football and Middle Eastern armies.

From *Management Today*, February 1993

Close to the Customer

There are two main reasons why being close to the customer is a major element in the growing entrepreneurial company. First, any company which is seeking to differentiate itself within its market must have a detailed knowledge of its customers and their existing and future needs. Secondly, close links to customers and markets will ensure that strategy development is market-based. The ability to spot trends and opportunities early and to keep ahead of the competition will depend on a detailed knowledge of customers' requirements and the major internal and external factors which are affecting their thinking. Flexibility and opportunism in strategic development are dependent upon being close to the customer.

It is important to understand what we mean by close to the customer. Many businesses would claim to be close to their customers but the reality is that their relationships are at arm's-length. The information flows between customer and supplier are on a "need to know" basis and the focus of thinking is on the requirements the customer has at any one time. In our view being close to the customer is about a much closer relationship, what Tom Peters calls "symbiosis with the customer". This involves:

- High levels of performance in meeting and beating customer needs
- Developing an understanding of customers' explicit and implicit needs
- Having the ability to come up with innovative solutions to customers' problems
- Having a platform to discuss future trends and developments
- Ongoing development and management of relationships.

This suggests a partnership where you are trying to make yourself indispensable to your customers by building loyalty based on commercial advantage to both partners. In doing this you will be strengthening your ability for increased business with your customers and be best placed to identify and capitalise on future changes and opportunities.

John Rehfeld has written about Japanese approaches to management and in particular he notes that the Japanese approach to customer service is based on the concept of *omoiyari*. This concept can be loosely translated as "filling anticipated needs" and involves an attitude which places the needs of customers first. According to Rehfeld, "*Omoiyari* shapes Japanese attitudes towards customer service" and this helps keep the management focused on understanding customers' needs and providing service excellence. This is the attitude and approach which permeates the successful entrepreneurial company.

Becoming *close to the customer* requires considerable effort and, given the resource constraints in any growing company, this will have a fundamental effect on the strategic focus of the business. If we are genuinely trying to create the type of relationships we have described, strategy development must be focused in creating closer links and better understanding of customer needs.

The creation of a strategic advantage will therefore depend upon building customer relationships and understanding needs, rather than concentrating on the activities of competitors. This is not to suggest that we ignore the activities of the competition but rather that our prime focus is in developing our relationships with customers and anticipating their needs. This suggests a dynamic approach to strategy where the emphasis is on leading rather than following. It means concentrating on customers and how you can satisfy them and letting competitors react to you, rather than deliberating on and second-guessing their anticipated moves.

A key issue in becoming close to your customers is understanding the value which you add to the relationship. Any business relationship is based on adding value. The more value you can add to your customer, the more valuable your relationship is. The concept of the value chain sees any business as a complex system which has inputs and outputs. The chain is made up of all the activities involved in the system: purchasing, manufacturing, distribution, sales and marketing, service and maintenance. You need to understand this concept in relation to your customers and the value which they add to their customers, as well as your customers' perceptions of the value you add to them. By doing this then you can start to identify how to move up this value chain and provide increased value to your customer.

Ramage Brothers, a highly successful haulage company, provides distribution services for major retailers by delivering electrical appliances to domestic customers. Initially this involved collecting the goods from the retailers' premises and delivering them to the customers. The company has increased the value which they provide to their customers by providing warehousing and stock ordering services, thus reducing their need for these facilities. It has also provided an increased level of service to the end user by training their drivers in setting up the electrical equipment and demonstrating to the customer how it should be used. In this way the company has become close to its customers by providing value added services.

In order to become *close to the customer* there are a number of actions which we need to take. These do not necessarily confine themselves to improving customer service.

Actions to Understand the Customer's Agenda

In order to satisfy customer needs we need to be able to understand what these needs are. Many companies make assumptions about customer needs based on a historical perspective and fall into the trap of thinking that these needs are static. Customer requirements and expectations are dynamic and we need to monitor changes in markets, lifestyles and trends. Keeping close to the customer involves knowing customer needs better than they do. Specific actions include:

- Regular customer questionnaires
- Focus groups with customers and their customers
- Ongoing product/service review meetings with customers
- Ongoing internal product/service review meetings
- Product/service development meetings
- Marketing research.

Actions to Bind Customers to You

If we are to create genuine partnerships with customers to give us a special relationship and an inside track on developments and opportunities then we must find creative and unique ways of adding value as well as providing a total service package which makes us indispensable. This can include:

- Swamping the customer with useful information
- Making it easy to do business with you through computer link-ups, user-friendly contracts, etc.
- Putting resources into educating customers
- Creating clubs to develop the customer as an insider
- Customisation of products and service
- Development of service contracts.

Developing Strategic Capability

Although market-based intuition, opportunism and flexibility can be seen as key entrepreneurial strengths in building businesses, entrepreneurial approaches to strategy development are not always successful.

Richard Buskirk has compiled a list of entrepreneurs' most serious early mistakes. The main ones identified were:

- Poor decisions about people's character
- Recruitment of individuals with inadequate skills
- Poor market judgement due to inadequate research
- Product, as opposed to market, orientation
- Inadequate growth strategy due to conservatism
- Inadequate growth strategy due to failure to spot trends early
- Inappropriate management style
- Poor timing of strategic decisions.

At least half of these mistakes relate to the area of strategic decision-making. This suggests that entrepreneurs recognise the importance of strategic decision-making in building successful companies and acknowledge that it is an area where mistakes are commonly made.

Our own experience suggests there are a number of common "traps" which entrepreneurs can easily fall into. These traps can blunt the strategic decision-making within the company and become a constraint to growth.

Entrepreneurial complacency. Here the early success of the entrepreneurial venture leads to a complacency about markets and customers which can blunt the decision-making ability.

Entrepreneurial infallibility. Having achieved a track record of success in one area, the entrepreneur believes that he has a "golden touch" in a number of unrelated ventures and activities.

Slow response to changing conditions. This is where the entrepreneur loses sight of the "big picture" because he is involved too heavily in the day-to-day operations of the business or has lost an element of the entrepreneurial drive and motivation.

Tunnel vision. A lack of openness and exposure to new ideas and the difficulty of being objective about the business can lock the entrepreneur into a fixed way of thinking which can be dangerous in a fast changing situation.

Over-reliance on intuition. Effective strategic thinkers regard the gathering and analysis of information as a prerequisite to decision-making and therefore although many entrepreneurs are good intuitive strategists their decisions must be based on analysis rather than simply "gut feel".

Missing out on opportunities. Carl Vesper has researched into the timing of when successful companies developed their "big idea" – the business concept on which the success was built. He suggests that only 24 per cent of companies had the main idea at start-up. Over 40 per cent of companies developed the key idea downstream from start-up. This demonstrates the importance of remaining flexible and opportunistic as the business develops.

We earlier described "tension in strategy" – the ability to balance opportunism with the requirement for enhanced thinking and planning in the area of strategy development – as a key aspect of the growing business. Strategy which is dependant upon intuition alone only has real value in the embryonic stages of business growth. After these phases the increasing complexity of the business and the momentum of the marketplace can overwhelm many intuitive strategists.

The successful entrepreneurial company is one where the strategic direction is continually questioned and tested. To do this effectively requires a high level of strategic awareness. The increasing complexity of the business, its markets and competitive situation, all call for the development of strategic thinking and the level of strategic planning within the business. This is particularly the case when the business reaches a stage when the entrepreneur needs to consider strategic growth options.

Strategic Growth Options

Gibb, in his studies into growth-orientated businesses, has suggested that the growing company tends to develop in discrete steps via a series of incremental product and market developments. This backs our own experience which suggests that entrepreneurs tend to take an incremental approach to building on what is already there, rather than the development of grand strategies and plans. However, there is a danger that this approach can be limiting unless there is a clear understanding of the strategic growth options and their implications for the business.

At any stage of business growth there is a need to recognise that major strategic decisions need to be faced about how the business extends itself beyond regional or small-scale trading. There are major strategic implications in addressing these issues as, in most cases, they suggest the need to develop new approaches to doing business.

Examples of strategic growth issues are:

- Development from being a niche player into other market areas where there is existing, established competition
- Move from a maturing market area into growth segments of the market
- Move from a small regional player to becoming a well established national player
- Maintaining a narrow product base and extending the geographic market
- Developing a brand or new distribution networks
- Extending into export markets while protecting the core market

These issues, and others like them, will provide a major strategic challenge to the business. They will need careful consideration and the development of a clearly thought-out strategy.

Many businesses do not grow beyond the development of a relatively small segment or geographic area. This is because the entrepreneur either lacks the motivation to develop the business on a larger scale, or is unable to create and implement a clear growth strategy to take the business forward. This is the stage where many entrepreneurs seek an exit. Recognising that they have built the business to the limit of their capabilities or aspirations, they start to look for a buyer.

Genuine growth entrepreneurs – those who wish to build substantial businesses – are able to tackle the issue of how they extend themselves beyond the limitations of existing markets or business approaches. Although flexibility and opportunism remain key aspects of building a business, successful growth entrepreneurs recognise the need for clarity in strategic thinking to ensure the development of a robust and highly informed growth strategy.

Although strategic thinking should be seen as a daily discipline, at certain stages of the business growth it is important to carry out a more formal process of strategic review which forces the management systematically to consider and evaluate options for growth and ongoing changes in the company's strategic situation. This is not to say that the entrepreneurs must emulate the strategic planning approaches of larger companies, but rather that they must improve the strategic decision-making process in a way which will complement the nature of the entrepreneurial company. This will happen only if entrepreneurs develop a high level of strategic awareness about the business and the environment in which it is operating.

The strategic triangle (see overleaf) is a key concept in business strategy that identifies the main elements which are involved in strategic decisions and for which the strategist must develop information. The strategic thinker understands the elements of this triangle and the interaction and interrelation of these elements in relation to their business. Strategic thinkers have the key elements of their strategy at the forefront of their thinking. This means that they are testing the strategy on an ongoing basis against any changes or potential changes affecting the circumstances of the business.

Although strategic thinking is a daily discipline there needs to more effective strategic planning by developing a framework which allows a

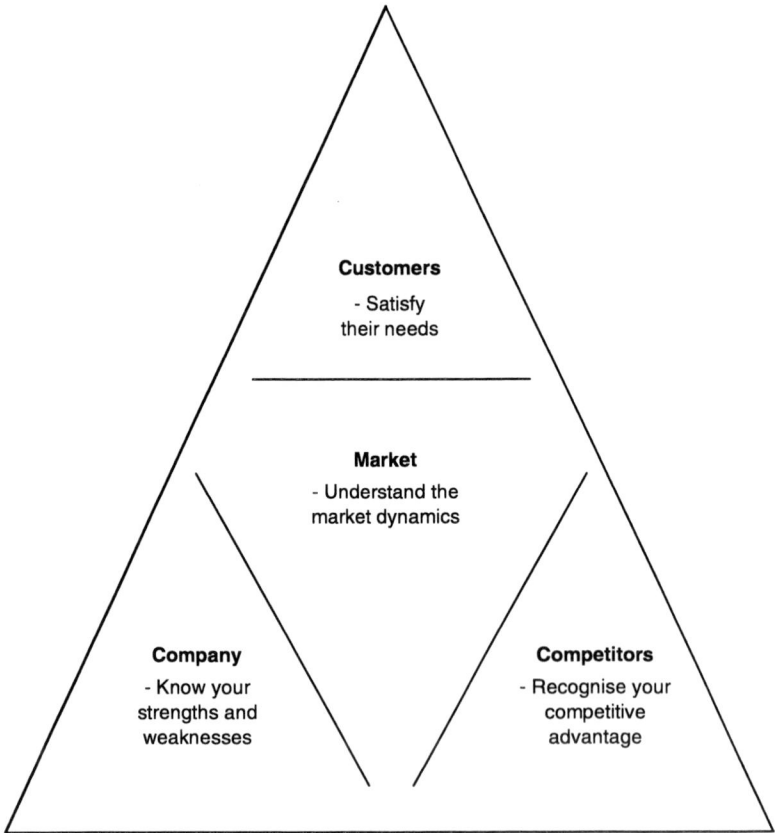

Strategic Triangle

regular, systematic review of the company's existing situation. Such reviews have a number of benefits:

- They offer an opportunity to review the progress of the business.
- They demand objective analysis of the business and its environment.
- They provide a focal point for future development.
- They provides an opportunity to fundamentally review key assumptions.
- They offer the opportunity to involve others in the strategic process.

142

This type of fundamental review should take place at least once a year and probably more frequently in a rapid growth company. They should not be seen as a replacement for the ongoing development of strategy, nor as an inhibitor to opportunism. Rather, they should be seen as a way of strengthening strategic awareness by giving a regular opportunity to fundamentally challenge and review the strategic focus of the business.

Flexibility and opportunism are key strengths which can give the entrepreneurial company an advantage within its markets. Therefore the strategic development process must reflect these strengths. Strategy must be seen as a living thing which has a constant goal but evolves in the light of changing conditions and emerging opportunities. This will happen only if strategy development is underpinned by innovative ways of doing business, niche thinking, increasing levels of strategic awareness and the ability to be close to the customer.

Chapter 8

Towards Enterprise – The Way Ahead

We started this book by suggesting that the entrepreneurial company was the natural model for an organisation which displays the flexibility and innovation necessary to develop and prosper in a time of ongoing market change. Over the time it has taken us to develop our thoughts and get them down on paper, there is increasing evidence to support our assertions.

In our study we have continued to work with entrepreneurs to help them grow their businesses and with larger organisations to encourage them to be more enterprising. It is obvious to us – in our company work and from the increased interest which is now being shown in entrepreneurs and entrepreneurial behaviour – that an increasing number of companies are aware of the potential benefits of making businesses more entrepreneurial.

In Chapter 1 we described a number of fallacies about the entrepreneurial company:

- All small companies are entrepreneurial.
- All entrepreneur-led companies are entrepreneurial.
- Entrepreneurs are born not made.
- As companies increase their size then entrepreneurship must diminish.

All too often we still come across many entrepreneurs and advisers who believe these statements and who propagate them through their attitudes and actions. More importantly, however, we have seen an increasing number of examples of entrepreneurs who recognise these statements as fallacies and have been working hard to dispel these myths in their own business situation.

All Small Companies Are Entrepreneurial

There appears to be an increasing understanding in many small companies that as they grow and set up a structure to support their development, there is a danger of losing the entrepreneurial traits which allowed them to become successful in the first place. The customer focus, the clarity of differentiation, the flexibility of action and the ability to be opportunistic, have all been diluted as the focus becomes increasingly towards internal rather than external development. Those companies which have recognised the danger have taken steps to make themselves more entrepreneurial by re-orienting their focus towards the customer and markets and developing structures and people that will encourage more enterprising behaviour.

All Entrepreneur-Led Companies Are Entrepreneurial

Many entrepreneurs are recognising that they may be a major stumbling block to the ongoing development of their company. Many entrepreneurs consistently underestimate the level of personal change which is required if they are to continue the development of their business. We have suggested that changes are required in leadership style and approach, attitudes towards others in the business as well as their role in the company. What is required is deep-rooted, fundamental change, but in many cases the entrepreneur is prepared only to make incremental change and accordingly the change does not have the desired impact in moving the company forward. Many founding entrepreneurs have large egos and can find it difficult to appreciate the level of personal change that is required and the degree of effort required to sustain such changes as the business grows.

We see evidence that much of the stimulus for change in entrepreneurs comes from external influences such as consultants, advisers and non-executive directors. In many cases, even where the need for change has been recognised by the entrepreneur, external influences can provide a stimulus for the necessary changes. Our own programme, Breakthrough Management, has encouraged entrepreneurs to review their own role and company situation to identify how they can move the business forward. Not surprisingly, many of the participants have recognised the importance of personal change and have suggested the programme was a major catalyst for stimulating a major change in their role.

Entrepreneurs Are Born Not Made

The strength of vision which is the supreme trait of the entrepreneurial type can be present at different stages in one's life and can be stimulated by different triggers or circumstances. This tends to create the notion that entrepreneurs are born, not made.

However, we believe that the question of whether entrepreneurs are born or made is not the main issue in developing entrepreneurial companies. Of more importance is understanding the distinctive aspects of entrepreneurial behaviour which set it apart from other types of behaviour. We have described a number of factors which made up the essential character of the entrepreneur and suggested that all of these would be present to a greater or lesser degree within the three broad descriptions of:

- Single-venture entrepreneur
- The growth entrepreneur
- The serial entrepreneur.

We were recently involved in a conference which brought together a group of entrepreneurs to talk about their business and share information. There was a wide mix of delegates – entrepreneurs who had sold their businesses for seven-figure sums, new-start entrepreneurs and those who were engaged in high growth companies. Every background was different and the reasons for setting up their businesses were many and varied. Each delegate had one thing in common: a wish to become more effective in building their businesses. Each delegate believed that they could become better entrepreneurs, and even those who had successfully built and sold their businesses recognised that many of the skills and attitudes they needed to build their companies had been shaped and developed over a long period of time.

As Companies Increase Their Size Then Entrepreneurship Must Diminish

Our programmes on intrapreneurship, where we have been developing enterprising behaviour in larger companies, have been a revelation to us about the latent entrepreneurial potential which is inherent in many larger companies. We have shown that many people, at all levels within the company, have the capacity to develop commercial ideas which can be developed into revenue streams for the business or major improvement areas. In one branch plant of a major multi-national we were able to work with the management to stimulate many ideas, each one with significant potential. This type of result can be achieved with the right leadership and a structure which provides a stimulus to release this latent potential.

In conclusion, we would like to reiterate the importance of increasing the level of entrepreneurship in the growing company and to reflect upon some of the key areas which demonstrate the level of entrepreneurial activity.

Our main theme is that if the entrepreneur is the focal point for the development of the entrepreneurial company, then we need to understand the existing entrepreneurial level of the leadership as a starting point in determining the entrepreneurial level of the company. The importance of the entrepreneur as the focal point for the growing company suggests that when entrepreneurial activity levels off it is probably because the leadership has become less entrepreneurial and allowed the business to become bogged down, or creeping bureaucracy has started to set in.

By assessing whether the level of entrepreneurial activity within the leadership of the business is increasing or diminishing we can tell whether there is a need for action to stimulate entrepreneurial activity. Reflecting upon the questions listed below will give some indication of the level of entrepreneurial activity within any company.

- **Is there a high level of new product/service activity?** If the culture is genuinely entrepreneurial then the company will be generating an ongoing stream of new product/service ideas. How many new product ideas has the company considered and successfully introduced over the past three years?

- **Is there a balance between freedom and control?** It is important to keep a balance between professionalising the business and keeping it entrepreneurial. Are the management becoming increasingly comfortable in a situation with increasing rules, controls and procedures which may be stifling innovation and slowing down decision-making?

- **Is there flexibility in strategic decision-making?** Have the leadership balanced the need for more formalised planning with an inherent flexibility in strategic thinking or has strategic planning or yearly budget setting become institutionalised within the business? When was the last time that a market opportunity (or threat) led to an unscheduled review of the strategic direction and a modification of the way of doing business?

- **Does the leadership regularly instigate a fundamental review of operations?** When was the last time that the overall activities, both internal and external, were fundamentally re-examined to identify those areas which were outworn? Did this review take the view that nothing is sacred and lead to radical change in major parts of the business?

- **How fast can the business react to a market opportunity?** If a key feature of entrepreneurial behaviour is to capitalise on opportunities, then speed of reaction is critical. Entrepreneurs follow the credo of "Ready, fire, aim" – which is why they are able to respond fast. When was the last time that you sacrificed complete knowledge about a situation for speed of reaction?

- **How quickly is the business aware of market opportunities?** Do you spot opportunities before others have capitalised on them or do you first become aware of them when someone else has introduced the product or service into the market?

- **Are the management stimulating new ventures?** New ventures can range from strategic alliances to joint ventures and can include spin-outs from the existing company and involvement in new start companies. How many innovative ventures have your company considered or become involved in recently?

- **Is the leadership developing innovative ways of getting close to the customer?** Entrepreneurial strategies should be underpinned by a closeness to customers and markets. This requires mechanisms for gathering and analysing customer information and feedback at all levels within the company and actions to align the company with customer needs.

Not surprisingly these questions relate to many of the characteristics of entrepreneurial companies which we have discussed throughout this book. It is our experience that many successful growing companies are becoming more entrepreneurial by raising horizons, bringing new ideas forward, stimulating spin-outs and new ventures and increasing all aspects of entrepreneurship within the business.

The entrepreneurs leading these companies are able to respond positively to the questions above and are shaping organisations which are characterised by a closeness to customers and markets, the encouragement of innovations, risk-taking and flexibility. Our hope for this book is that it adds to the emerging understanding of the art of entrepreneurship. We also hope that these insights will help many others to shape a more entrepreneurial company.

Bibliography

Burch, John G, *Entrepreneurship*, John Wiley & Sons, 1986

Drucker, Peter, *Innovation and Entrepreneurship,* Heinemann, 1985

Handy, Charles, *The Empty Raincoat*, Century Business,1992

McClelland, Douglas C, *The Achieving Society*, Tree Press, 1967

Mintzberg, Henry, *The Rise and Fall of Strategic Planning*, Prentice Hall, 1994

Mumford, A, *Making Experience Pay*, McGraw-Hill, 1980

Lewis, Ken, and Lytton, Stephen, *How to Transform Your Company and Enjoy It*, Management Books 2000, 1995

Nayak, P R, and Ketteringham, John, *Breakthroughs!*, Management Books 2000, 1993

Neumann, Jean, Holti, Richard, and Standing, Hilary, *Change Everything At Once!*, Management Books 2000, 1995

Ohmae, Kenichi, *The Mind of the Strategist,* McGraw-Hill, 1982

Peters, Tom, *Liberation Management,* Macmillan Press, 1992

Pinchot III, Gifford, *Intrapreneuring*, Harper and Row, 1985

Power, Daniel, "Anticipating Organisation Structure" in *Futures of Organisations*, J Hage (Ed), Lexington Books, 1988

Rehfeld, J E, *Alchemy of a Leader*, John Wiley & Sons, 1994

Roberts, E, *Entrepreneurship in High Technology*, 1991

Rotler, J B, "External Central and Internal Control", *Psychology Today*, June 1971

Sadler, P, *Designing Organisations*, Mercury, 1991

Slevin & Covin, "Juggling Organisational Style and Structure", *Sloan Management Review*, Winter 1990

Index